A Teacher's Guide to the Psychology of Learning

Second Edition

A Teacher's Guide to the Psychology of Learning

SECOND EDITION

Michael J. A. Howe

Exeter University

Copyright © Michael J. A. Howe 1984, 1999

The right of Michael J. A. Howe to be identified as author of this work has been asserted in accordance with the Copyright, Designs and Patents Act 1988.

First published 1984
Reprinted 1986, 1988, 1989, 1991, 1992, 1993 (twice), 1995, 1998
Second edition published 1999

2 4 6 8 10 9 7 5 3 1

Blackwell Publishers Ltd
108 Cowley Road
Oxford OX4 1JF
UK

Blackwell Publishers Inc.
350 Main Street
Malden, Massachusetts 02148
USA

British Library Cataloguing in Publication Data

A CIP catalogue record for this book is available from the British Library.

Library of Congress Cataloging-in-Publication Data
Howe, Michael J. A., 1940–
    A teacher's guide to the psychology of learning/Michael J. A. Howe. — 2nd ed.
        p.   cm.
    Includes bibliographical references (p.   ) and index.
    ISBN 0-631-21226-4 (alk. paper). — ISBN 0-631-21227-2 (pbk. : alk. paper)
    1. Educational psychology.   2. Learning, Psychology of.   3. Cognition in
children.   I. Title.
LB1051.H79296   1999
370.15'23—dc21   98-47770
                                                                               CIP

Typeset in 10½ /12½ pt Bembo
by Ace Filmsetting Ltd, Frome, Somerset
Printed in Great Britain by M. P. G. Books Ltd, Bodmin, Cornwall

This book is printed on acid-free paper

Contents

Preface

This is the second edition of *A Teacher's Guide to the Psychology of Learning*. I began the preface to the first edition by saying that all teachers should be experts in human learning. I pointed out that, as well as having practical expertise, teachers need to know about those scientific advances in knowledge of the mechanisms and causes of learning that can be applied to the vital job of helping children and adolescents to learn.

In common with the earlier edition, the second edition draws upon the contributions of modern cognitive psychology to our understanding of those kinds of learning that are needed for making progress in the school classroom. This book, like the previous one, concerns itself with the acquisition of the cognitive abilities that enable a young student to become educated. The emphasis is on the learning of intellectual skills and forms of knowledge that are based on language, and there is stress on the kinds of basic skills that make literacy and numeracy possible.

In planning the new edition, my original aim was to make only modest changes to the previous one, updating the content but making few other alterations. However, as I began work it quickly became apparent that the changes needed to be far more substantial than I had envisaged. Consequently, a number of the chapters in this second edition are entirely new, and although most of the other chapters make use of material from the earlier edition, the majority have been much altered.

Michael J. A. Howe,
October 1998.

1

Introduction: The Beginnings of Human Learning

Learning is what we humans do. In the past it allowed our species to survive, making us unusually adaptable. That enabled humans to cope with massive changes in climate and geography that would have defeated many other animals. Learning furnishes our minds with the skills and capabilities that we depend upon. Without it, life as an independent adult is inconceivable.

There are many forms and varieties of learning, some of which we share with other species, but humans are set apart from other animals by having the capacity to acquire language. In this we are quite unique, for there is nothing remotely like human language in any other species. Language makes possible numerous kinds of competence that could not even be imagined in a species lacking it. As well as allowing us to communicate with other people, language allows us to talk to ourselves, to think and reason, and make conscious choices. Language enables us to store and have access to huge quantities of information. It permits us to remember the past and make plans for the future.

Rather than imagining learning as being a single process, it would be more realistic to think of the word 'learning' as a term that refers to a broad range of mental events in the mind. These differ in various ways but they share some common elements. For instance, all forms of learning involve change taking place in the individual learner. Often, but by no means always, the change is evident in a person's behaviour. In many cases an alteration that learning brings about helps to extend the individual's capacities. However, learning can be maladaptive as well as adaptive (Howe, 1975, 1980).

When we learn something new we are frequently conscious of doing so, but sometimes we are not at all aware of the detailed changes learning has brought. By way of illustration, gaining the capability to juggle wooden balls or other objects expertly involves an enormous feat of learning, and yet a skilled juggler cannot report on the precise changes that took place as she gradually mastered the skill.

The fact that the single term 'learning' refers to a variety of mental events makes it impossible to have a single precise definition of learning. However, practically all forms of learning take the form of acquired changes in individual people. Within education, many of the kinds of learning that are especially important have the effect of helping young people to extend their capacities in one way or another (Fontana, 1981). Typically, those kinds of learning that contribute to success at school and are of particular interest to teachers and educators are ones that depend upon human language. Even in those forms of learning where there is no obvious necessity for language, such as the acquisition of sporting skills or expertise at playing a musical instrument, language often does have a substantial role in training and instruction.

In this book I concentrate on forms of learning that are specifically human and make a fairly direct contribution to the gains in capabilities that are associated with education. Less attention is given to certain forms of learning that have been extensively studied in other animals, such as various kinds of conditioning. These kinds of learning are not unknown in humans, and are certainly not unimportant, but since language-based kinds of learning play a more direct role in bringing about the kinds of changes that contribute to a young person becoming educated, these have been given priority.

Much language-based learning involves the acquisition of new information or knowledge. When people are discussing the acquisition of knowledge they sometimes introduce the word 'remember' rather than 'learn'. These two words are often used interchangeably, but in the following pages it is best to assume that the appearance of one or other term reflects a deliberate choice of one over the other. It is certainly not true that the different words imply distinct mental processes or separate underlying mechanisms. And in common with the word 'learning', each of the terms 'memory' and 'remembering' refers to a range of phenomena. Note also that, while it is true that retaining or remembering information is an important function of the human brain, the idea that people possess one unitary memory is an oversimplification. A substantial number of brain processes and mechanisms contribute in one way or another to a person's capacity to retain and retrieve stored information. Remembering is crucial, but doing it requires the combined efforts of a number of mental systems.

Of course, learning does not begin with school. The child who arrives at school for the very first time is in many respects already an expert learner, having gained many vital capabilities, including language, as well as the numerous items of knowledge that a 5-year-old depends upon. Starting school is an important transition and sometimes a difficult one, because in the school environment the child is required to engage in learning in circumstances that may be very different from ones that have been encountered previously.

Learning in the Earliest Years

Certain kinds of simple learning can take place even prior to birth (Hepper, 1991). However, the prenatal environment has its limitations: its darkness precludes forms of learning that depend upon vision, and the fact that access to sounds from the world outside is somewhat limited forms another severe restriction. So it is not until birth that the baby comes into contact with circumstances that are really ideal for learning.

Once born, babies soon start taking advantage of opportunities to learn (Karmiloff-Smith, 1995). They quickly get on with it, despite the incomplete development of their brains. That learning has taken place is evident, for example, in a child aged four weeks whose hungry cries begin to stop just before his mother picks him up to feed him. It is clear that the child has already formed a mental connection between feeding and his mother's actions: previous experience has taught him that food is to be expected. That learning has occurred can be confirmed by observing that the child's cries increase again if the mother now walks away without picking the child up.

Another child usually goes on crying after she has been picked up, but she begins to be calmer when her mother takes her into the room where she will be fed. Again, it is clear that this child has, through learning, made a mental connection, in this case between having food and being in a particular room. Also, a newborn who hears the identical sound every time she starts to receive milk will soon start sucking if the sound occurs on its own, demonstrating that the baby has learned to link those two events. In these cases it is clear that the baby is already learning and that learning is making a real contribution to the child's life. It brings some order and predictability to events which at the time of birth would have been perceived as no more than random happenings.

Babies begin life outside the womb reasonably well-equipped to take advantage of opportunities to learn. At birth they can already perceive patterns and have a preference for human faces, as well as being able to hear and smell. They soon start exploring their world, turning towards objects to bring them into focus as early as the first week, moving their heads in response to sounds and using their mouths to investigate new objects. They quickly learn to connect voices and faces, so that a child aged one month may become upset at hearing the mother's voice coming from somewhere other than her face. And as early as the first week babies can learn to vary their rate of sucking in order to get a reward – hearing the mother's voice.

By around four months a baby will be starting to enjoy the experience of making things happen, gaining obvious pleasure from the achievement of making a noise, or moving a toy, or knocking it down. The child is beginning to gain some control and mastery, starting out on the long journey towards independence.

So even in the first six months it is clear that babies are active learners, and depend upon learning in order to make good progress. Not surprisingly, research studies have demonstrated that babies who are attentive and keen to explore often grow into unusually capable young children, and infants who are good at concentrating are likely to become able youngsters.

Language and Human Learning

Much of the learning that young humans do in their earliest years is not very different from forms of learning that can also be observed in other mammals, such as the *conditioning* whereby animals form connections between important events, and the *imitative learning* that extends a young animal's repertoire of actions, and also the various *habituation* phenomena that function to ensure that a young individual pays closer attention to new and potentially crucial happenings than to repeated ones that can often be ignored with impunity. But from an early stage babies begin to gain knowledge and skills that will contribute to the acquisition of language. Although children do not actually begin to talk until around the end of the first year, well before that time they begin gaining capabilities that will help to make language possible, active speech being the end product of much language learning, not its beginning.

Babies whose parents regularly talk to them learn communication skills that language builds upon, learning how to make the sounds that language uses, and discovering that sounds can represent objects and experiences. Well before they start talking, babies gain plenty of practice at communicating with other people, and the games that parents play with their babies provide plenty of practice at the kind of turn-taking activities – involving alternatively attending to another person and actively responding oneself – that are central to the ability to take part in a conversation.

Early communicative abilities provide a foundation that spoken language builds upon. Speech becomes a possibility after a child has progressed through various pre-language phases. Humans are able to acquire language only because their brains have evolved to make this possible. That does not necessarily mean that people are born possessing specific mechanisms for acquiring language rules, as was proposed by Noam Chomsky. However, it is not true that any intelligent animal with a large brain is capable of gaining language through a process of associative learning, as was claimed by one prominent psychologist, B. F. Skinner, in the 1950s. Although some primates have been taught a vocabulary of correspondences between objects and tokens or words that signify them, only humans appear to be capable of the kind of symbolic learning that is basic to structured language (Deacon, 1997). Human brains, unlike those of other animals, possess mechanisms that make it possible for language to be learned, and this accounts for the fact that virtually all humans do acquire at least the rudiments of a language, whereas attempts to teach language to other species have not been successful.

It has sometimes been asserted that there is little or no point in deliberately assisting children to acquire their native language, since most children eventually do gain language with even minimal encouragement. However, learning one's own language is not an all-or-nothing matter. It is important to recognize that although even deprived and neglected children eventually gain some language skills, they are nevertheless handicapped. That is because their limited linguistic capabilities may be insufficient for life in a complex contemporary society. The possession of good language skills opens many doors and transforms a child's capacity to think and remember. Delayed language development, in contrast, leads to restrictions in mastering the reasoning and planning capabilities that language makes possible.

Giving formal training in a child's own language can be counter-productive, and it has been observed that overemphasis on eliminating grammatical mistakes can actually impede a child's progress. All the same, parental encouragement can have substantial positive effects. The sheer amount of talk by parents is not crucial, but children are more likely to develop good language capabilities if their parents talk to them frequently and are responsive to their baby's early efforts to communicate (Fowler, 1990; Hart and Risley, 1995). Children especially benefit from speech that is specifically directed towards them and refers to objects and experiences that are already engaging their attention. Language development prospers when parents talk with their children rather than at them, and create plenty of opportunities in which parent and child can each respond to the other.

As early as the fourth month there may be real progress towards understanding language, and soon after the sixth month a baby may demonstrate some genuine language comprehension. This is apparent, for example, when a baby's response to the mother's 'Where's Daddy?' is to turn towards the door. By the end of the first year a child may comprehend as many as twenty or so different words, and repeatedly utter sounds that are clear enough for the parents to recognize as being words.

Broadly speaking, young children are most likely to thrive as young learners when their parents are not only conscientious in providing plenty of stimulation but also take pains to be sensitive and attuned to the particular temperament and personality of their child. Effective learning sessions for young children are usually informal ones, often involving some kind of game or play activity. It is sensible for parents to regard themselves more as guides than as teachers. As guides, parents help their children to make sense of the world, drawing a child's attention to events and objects that are particularly significant, aware of the child's restricted knowledge and understanding, and making a real effort to see things from the child's point of view. Children benefit when their parents not only engage in plenty of activities that involve them but also make an effort to include them in many aspects of daily life, sharing everyday experiences and encouraging the child to participate in regular activities such as shopping and cooking. Effective parents are also careful to ensure that there are times when a child is given all the parent's attention.

Children have limited attention spans and are easily distracted. Wise parents should never persist in trying to maintain a child's interest in an activity when the child has signalled that he or she is fatigued or bored. Criticism is never helpful and can easily discourage a child; even the intense enthusiasm of a parent eager to teach their children new things can put a child off, appearing to the child as a kind of pressure. On occasion it is a good idea for parents to rein in their eagerness to promote learning and consciously adopt a laid-back approach, keeping things playful as well as informal, and never too intense.

In the course of the earliest years a child gradually acquires a repertoire of learned skills, capabilities and knowledge that can be drawn upon later, making further development possible and forming a basis on which more advanced abilities can build. However, in the years that follow babyhood, those that immediately precede starting school, a range of further skills are acquired that make a direct contribution to the chances of a young person's schooldays being fruitful and successful as far as learning is concerned. Some of the forms of learning that take place in the years immediately preceding learning will be examined in the following chapter.

Finally, in order for a young child to become a good learner during the later years it is not enough to have knowledge and skills alone: the young person also needs to gain broader habits that help to maximize learning. That is demonstrated by the findings of a study which started by assessing 4-year-olds according to the extent to which they were capable of delaying gratification, by choosing to resist the temptation of a small immediate reward in favour of a larger reward that could be obtained if the child was prepared to wait for a short time (Shoda, Mischel and Peake, 1990). These researchers confronted the 4-year-olds who participated in their study with a choice. Either they could have a treat in the form of a marshmallow immediately, or they could wait while the researcher left the room in order to do an errand and subsequently returned, and be given two marshmallows rather than one.

Unsurprisingly, some of the children were able to wait and received the larger reward, while others found it impossible to delay gratification in this way. But what makes the study particularly interesting is that the researchers were able to examine the possibility of a relationship between the manner in which the children had dealt with this challenge – at the age of 4 – and the same children's progress many years later. This study was made possible because the researchers succeeded in tracking down the same children towards the end of their schooling.

It was discovered that, years later, there were striking differences between the individuals who, as 4-year-olds, had succeeded in delaying gratification and those who had not done so. As adolescents, those who had resisted temptation in the earlier study were better able to deal with frustrations, more competent socially and more self-assertive. They were also better at resisting pressure and more effective at persisting at challenges rather than giving up when they did not immediately succeed. They were more self-reliant and dependable, and more trustworthy. They were better at taking initiative. In short, as independent learners, they had made considerably more progress towards maturity. In contrast, the individuals who had not been able to delay gratification as young children were having a harder time at school, experiencing more difficulties and being less self-confident and more immature.

Toward the end of schooling, the two groups were compared on the basis of their academic accomplishments. Once again, success at delaying gratification at the age of 4 was a good predictor of later success, with the resisters having appreciably higher scores than the others on tests of both language–based and mathematical capabilities.

What do these findings mean? The obvious implication – that acquiring a capacity to stick with a task and resist temptations early in life gives a child inevitable advantages – is not the only possibility, although it may well be partly correct. It is equally likely that one of the reasons for the children's behaviour at the age of 4 being a good predictor of their competence much later was that broadly the same background circumstances that led to a child acting maturely at the age of 4 would have been in place throughout the same individual's childhood. For example, it is likely that the young children who delayed gratification successfully would have had caring and attentive parents who encouraged them to be relatively independent and mature in their activities. And the same home and family background features that influenced a child at 4 would have remained in place in the following years. So it is reasonable to believe that the reason why the children who could delay gratification were still doing well many years later was not just because acquiring at an early age the capacity to delay directly resulted in superior development, but also because their capacity to delay was an *indicator* that a child was being brought up in a favourable home background. And there are also other possible contributing reasons to the relationship between a child's maturity at the age of 4 and the same child's progress in the following years.

Most importantly, however, what the study shows is that early skills as such are not the only influences that contribute to a child's continuing mental development. Those broader aspects of personality and temperament that contribute to making a child act in a mature manner when confronting tasks and challenges are also important, perhaps equally so.

2

— Preparing for Learning at School —

The child who arrives at school for the first time is by no means new to the business of learning. Any young person of this age will already have notched up some massive learned achievements, and will have become a highly experienced learner in some respects. But although all 5- and 6-year-olds are capable learners, children do vary considerably in the extent to which their lives before school have prepared them for the particular kinds of learning that are crucial in school education. Two children at the beginning of their school careers may be equally quick, intelligent and well-informed, and yet they may differ enormously in the extent to which what they have learned at home has prepared them to do well in the new and unfamiliar learning environment that is encountered at school.

Learning at Home and Learning at School

School learning is different in many ways from the learning that takes place out of school. For most children there are major differences between school and home in both the kinds of things that are learned and the forms of learning that are emphasized. There are also important differences in the circumstances in which learning occurs. School makes many demands upon the young learner that are different from those typically experienced in everyday life at home.

Language is undoubtedly important at home as well as at school as a medium of communication. At school, however, language alone has to carry burdens which at home are shared between language and other aids to learning. For example, the teacher may have to rely exclusively on language to give information or communicate instructions to a fairly large number of children. The beginning student may be more familiar with one-to-one learning situations, in which the mother who teaches her child is able to supplement language with non-verbal communication, often using facial expressions. A mother can also demonstrate things to her child or intervene in various ways if she thinks her child needs assistance (Wachs and Gruen, 1982). For a teacher faced with a large number of children in the classroom, this is less likely to be possible.

School gives prominence to the acquisition of intellectual skills and knowledge rather than movement-based abilities, to abstract and symbolic achievements rather than concrete ones, and to abilities that are necessary for long-term achievements rather than ones which have immediate practical value for the learner. Learning in school is very often deliberate, involving a definite intention to learn or remember. At home, on the other hand, it is less usual for a child to engage in an activity with the express purpose of learning or remembering something. Consequently, despite all that he has learned, the pre-school child may not be at all familiar with the meaning of sentences like 'Try to learn this' or 'I want you to remember. . .', which a teacher may introduce without being aware that those words are not going to be meaningful to all children.

For many children, it is only when school begins that it becomes necessary to set out to learn information or acquire skills that are not closely bound to ongoing activities, or to confront a task in which learning is the explicit goal. Furthermore, for large numbers of children, those kinds of learning tasks that make it necessary for the individual to have definite plans or strategies for learning or remembering are first encountered at school.

So even without concentrating on those skills that are closely associated with schooling as such, including ones that directly contribute to literacy and numeracy, it is easy to see that, despite all the child's experience as a learner, some unfamiliar and difficult challenges must be faced when school begins. Even for the best-prepared child, learning at school is not simply a continuation of home life. Its demands are new and difficult.

Imagine yourself in the position of a child going to school for the very first time. Here are some specific ways in which you might find that school is different from anything you have previously experienced:

1   First, at school it can be hard to find an adult to help you when you need assistance. That is because there so many other children. Rather than being able to count on getting plenty of adult attention from a caring parent, you have to share one adult with a number of other children. You cannot expect quick responses to your requests for help.

2   With no familiar parents around, you have to deal with a stranger who is struggling to get to know the numerous children in the classroom.

3   It is likely that you will be asked, perhaps for the first time, to learn and remember things for their own sake. Unlike what happens at home, the learning activities you are asked to do may not have an obvious reason or purpose. There almost certainly is a reason for learning, but it may be hidden from you. A teacher may begin to start a new and unfamiliar topic just by saying, 'Today we are all going to learn about. . .' without saying why.

4   At school you are expected to concentrate on what your teacher says. At the same time it may be necessary to shut out various distractions from noisy children in the classroom. When you are at home, your parents will usually notice if you do not do what they are saying, or do not understand. Usually they will repeat what they have said when they see the need. At school this is unlikely to happen.

5   At school you may have to vary your pace and adjust the timing of your activities, according to the requirements of the teacher. She in turn will be concerned by the pace set by other children. That creates other differences from what happens at home, where you can usually set your own pace. At home, too, if you become tired or bored with one activity it is usually possible to do

something else. At school, however, that may not be permitted.

6 You may be expected to engage in various activities that are totally unfamiliar, and at the same time difficult and apparently pointless. Or you may be very unsure about exactly what it is that you are supposed to be doing. And since the help you need may be slow to arrive, because the teacher cannot attend to a number of children at the same time, it is hardly surprising that you may find yourself thoroughly confused and doing everything wrongly.

7 Adding to the feelings of frustration you experience when you find things confusing and difficult, you may discover that other children are making better progress than you are. And if there is an element of competition in the culture of the school classroom, you may soon begin to experience a feeling of failing.

Naturally, teachers make a big effort to ease children into the new learning environment of school and try to minimize the difficulties. Teachers are also fully aware that differences in previous experiences make children unequally prepared for the kinds of learning tasks that youngsters encounter at school. There is a limit, however, to what is humanly possible within the constraints of an average school classroom. Even with the best teacher in the world, the child whose home experiences have not prepared him well for school will almost inevitably be at an disadvantage, compared with another young person.

As we have seen, even when the home backgrounds of two children have been equally loving and supportive, the degree to which life at home has prepared them for the particular demands and challenges of school may be very unequal. Within the culture of the school it is natural to place stress on those kinds of learning that are based on language and symbols, writing and written knowledge. Other kinds of learning receive less emphasis. So a child who has good language skills, some knowledge of letters and words and a degree of basic competence with numbers, will be better prepared for the classroom than a child whose home learning experiences have not given much attention to those particular skills.

Reading

Reading stands out among all the school attainments that are crucial for success at both school and in life outside school, and which are strongly influenced by the kinds of preparatory learning experiences that a child receives at home, before starting school. Of all the capabilities that are (usually) acquired at school, reading is arguably the most important. Among its other consequences, acquiring the ability to read makes a learner much more independent and self-sufficient than before. Access to stored knowledge becomes possible. Children who can read can find out all kinds of things for themselves, and are capable of obtaining various kinds of information that are inaccessible to non-readers. Young people who are readers are already in control of important aspects of their own lives.

Learning to read is a major achievement for any child or adult. It is difficult. In order to read it is necessary for a person to acquire a variety of simpler skills and to internalize a substantial amount of knowledge. A child has to bring together various acquired capabilities in order to meet the changing demands of reading tasks.

It is not at all unexpected that many learners experience major problems with learning to read. In reality it would be far more surprising if difficulties were uncommon. There are many possible reasons for a child experiencing problems. Because mastering reading is a complex and difficult challenge, it is all too easy for learners to go wrong, and many young learners do indeed have failures. That is almost inevitable.

There is a common tendency to attach a label – 'dyslexic' – to virtually any child who does not succeed in learning to read at the usual age. That is a regrettable practice, because this label gives the misleading impression that every child who experiences serious difficulties must have some specific deficit. In fact this is far from being the case. The vast majority of children who have difficulty learning to read do so simply because, for some reason or other, they fail to master certain of the numerous capabilities that reading draws upon. In short, they fail because it is so easy to fail at reading.

In a small minority of those children who fail to learn to read their failure is related to specific defects, and in these few cases the introduction of the word 'dyslexia' is justified, with the term carrying the implication that behind the failure to learn reading there is some specific underlying condition. But with the vast majority of children who experience difficulties the implication that there is a particular known cause of their problems is unhelpful. It is unhelpful for the same reason that it would not be at all useful to attach a label to those individuals who experience problems in, say, learning to drive, or learning to knit or to cook. In the latter instances, the reasonable assumption is that the best way to help someone who experiences problems is to provide further opportunities to perfect those essential skills that have not yet been mastered. In many cases, exactly the same kind of approach is most likely to be helpful in cases of failure to learn to read.

Some research findings illustrate both the damaging effects upon reading of a lack of certain basic skills and the benefits of ensuring that a would-be reader does possess those skills. Among the capabilities whose absence makes learning to read practically impossible are ones that enable a child to identify sounds precisely and detect small differences that are crucial when listening to words. It is particularly important to perceive and be aware of the smallest sound units of language, *phonemes*. A child who does not perceive phonemes accurately will not be capable of discriminating between two different phonemes (such as the *b* in *bad* and the *d* in *dad*), and consequently will find it extremely difficult to learn to read.

In one study (Bradley and Bryant, 1983; Bryant and Bradley, 1985), the researchers asked 4- and 5-year-olds to listen to lists of around three words. In two of those words there was a common phoneme. The task for the child task was to say which was the odd word out. It was discovered that 4-year-olds' level of performance at this task was a good predictor of the same children's achievements at reading and spelling four years later. That finding seems to confirm that there exists a connection between possessing phonological skills in early childhood and making good progress at learning to read.

If that is indeed true, giving young children extra opportunities to practice discriminating between phonemes might help them to avoid certain reading difficulties later on. Does that happen? To examine that possibility, Bradley and Bryant carried out a further investigation. The participants were 65 children who did poorly at the phoneme discrimination task. These children, as the previous experiment had established, were ones who were likely to make restricted progress as readers.

The children were divided into four groups. Two groups were given training in listening to sounds and categorizing them. The training was not particularly time-consuming: each child attended twenty ten-minute sessions per year, for two years. Groups 1 and 2 were given fairly similar training: in Group 1 the children learned to discriminate between similar phoneme sounds, and the Group 2 children received the same instruction but were also taught to associate letter sounds with actual letters. Those children who formed Group 3 were taught to discriminate between categories. However, their training did not include discriminating between sounds. Group 4 formed a control condition, in which the children received no instruction at all.

All the participants were tested when they had reached the age of 8 years. By this time the children who had been allocated to Group 4, and who had received no special training at all, were lagging a year behind the normal standard of achievement at reading. At spelling, too, they were two years below average. The children in Group 3, who had received training in making discriminations, but not ones that involved phonemes, were also below average at tests of reading and spelling. In contrast, the child participants who had been allocated to each of the two groups who received training discriminating between phonemes were doing much better. Those participants who formed Group 1 were slightly below average at reading, and worse at spelling. However, the children who had formed Group 2, and who had been trained to discriminate between different phonemes and to make associations between sounds and letters were not at all below average. Despite their initial handicap, they were successfully reading at the expected level for children of their age.

The findings of these and other investigations confirm that

ensuring that children are good at discriminating between the sounds they hear, by providing training in basic skills involving listening to letters, sounds and phonemes, considerably reduces the likelihood that a child will experience difficulties in learning to read. Similarly, the results of another investigation showed that training young children to break words down into their constituent sounds and blend sounds together produced large gains in reading (Goldstein, 1976).

Reading is not the only area of ability in which it is likely that learning problems which actually arise as a result of a lack of basic skills are wrongly attributed to a specific condition or disability. In the same way that many of the problems that have led to children being called 'dyslexic' stem from adults' failure to notice that certain essential fundamental skills have not been gained, the belief that a child suffers from so-called 'learning disabilities' may in some cases be rooted in a similar failure to notice that essential basic skills have not been acquired. Thus,

> Teachers often erroneously assume that children entering school have 'prerequisite' reading skills developed as part of preschool maturation . . . These children have 'deficits' in learning certain reading skills because they simply have no experience with them and because schools, erroneously assuming children should already have these skills, do not teach them. (Coles, 1987, p. 54)

In the case of reading, formal pre-school training in listening skills will not normally be necessary so long as a child's home background provides reasonably rich experiences related to listening to language, and providing that the parents regularly read to a child and encourage activities such as rhyming and other language games. Children who regularly enjoy home experiences of reading and language are less likely than others to experience serious difficulties with learning to read (Moon and Wells, 1979; Whitehurst and Valdez-Menchaca, 1988; Whitehurst et al., 1988).

Learning in Modern Life

As children get older, they learn more and more about how to do well at the kinds of learning to which school gives emphasis. With learning becoming an increasingly deliberate kind of activity, young people discover how to plan their learning activities and make use of various procedures and strategies, such as rehearsing and practising, which are discussed in later chapters. It is sometimes argued that school learning is often artificial or unnatural, in the sense of not being immediately relevant to the child's here-and-now experience of daily living. That is true up to a point, but on the other hand to some extent it has to be, if it is to prepare people for adult life in modern societies. By the standards of primitive man the modern world is indeed artificial and unnatural. Stone-age people did not have to be greatly concerned with numeracy or literacy, and today's schooling would not have had much direct value for their everyday lives. But today's world is different, and we do have to be literate and numerate in order to enjoy fulfilling lives. Of course, in a fast-changing world there is always the danger that the content of school education will become removed from the concerns of the world outside school, a possibility that was wittily parodied sixty years ago in a book called *The Sabre-Tooth Curriculum* (Benjamin, 1939), and educators do have to make sure that what is taught in school does have relevance to the lives of the pupils.

Older children are generally more successful than younger ones at learning and remembering, but we should not jump to the conclusion that becoming older automatically leads to improvements. To a considerable extent, the fact that older individuals do better is not an automatic consequence of human development, but an outcome of the fact that because the older a person is the larger the number of learning experiences and opportunities he or she will have been exposed to, in much the same way that the older a person is the more likely it is that he or she will have enjoyed the experience of getting drunk, having measles or eating oysters. Also, much learning builds cumulatively on previous learning. Consequently, for example, a young student will be unable to master algebra until some progress has been made at basic arithmetic.

In practice, therefore, older individuals do have big advantages as learners. All the same, acknowledging the fact that the older person's advantages are largely learned ones rather than being inevitable or automatic consequences of getting older does have some important implications. It means, for example, that we would be wrong to assume that the reason one boy's failure at algebra is 'because he is not old enough', or to think that another pupil cannot learn to read simply because she is insufficiently mature, with the implication that all the teacher can do is to wait for the right time to arrive. If young children are consistently failing at tasks that give older children no trouble, it is at least worth trying to discover what it is that makes older children more successful, and then attempting to teach the young children to follow the procedures that older individuals draw upon.

There is every reason to believe that a substantial number of the mental skills, strategies, methods and procedures that older people make use of to their advantage can fairly readily be acquired by young children, if they are given suitable instruction. The belief that a child's mental capabilities are fixed or rigidly restricted by age-related limits is not one that is supported by hard factual evidence.

Not all developmental psychologists would agree with that point of view. Some would argue that it is inconsistent with the classical 'stage' theory that was originally advanced by the great Swiss psychologist Jean Piaget. According to that theory, the structures in the brain that underlie the mental operations which are necessary for reasoning, learning and solving problems that depend upon thinking advance through a series of fixed stages, with developmental progress occurring in steps, in the way we would associate with moving up a staircase, as opposed to proceeding along a steady upward slope. Some developmental psychologists would insist that a child's achievements are firmly limited by the stage he or she has reached. An implication of that viewpoint is that, if a particular ability is one which requires that the child has reached a more advanced stage, there is no point in trying to teach that skill on its own until the necessary stage has been reached. Moreover, it is argued by some developmental psychologists in the Piagetian tradition that advancing from one stage to another cannot readily be achieved through specific instances of learning: a broad variety of experiences is necessary.

Opposing that point of view is a large body of evidence showing that young children are actually able to learn many things which, if all the above statements about stages in mental development were correct, they would not be able to acquire. For example, Charles Brainerd (1977) demonstrated that it is entirely possible for the acquisition of concepts that involve a transition from one of Piaget's stages to a higher stage to be achieved by normal learning mechanisms. Therefore, so long as necessary prerequisite skills are either available to a child or can be taught, there is no fundamental reason, Brainerd asserted, why a child cannot learn those abilities which Piaget considered to denote a higher stage of mental development.

Although the contribution of Piaget to our understanding of child development is still very highly regarded, many psychologists today agree with Brainerd that the progress of young children is not so closely linked to fixed stages as Piaget and his followers believed (see, for example, Meadows, 1996). Research studies have shown that certain failures by young children at various reasoning tasks, which were once thought to provide justification for the belief that there are definite stages in mental development that sharply constrain learning, are actually due to other causes. These other causes include a child's inability to understand the language used in instructions, and the failure to see the point of a question.

In a number of experiments, it has been found that, when pains have been taken to ensure that the child definitely understands the instructions and perceives the task as being meaningful and interesting, young children are indeed capable of feats that, according to Piaget, ought to be impossible for them (Donaldson, 1978). And it has also been suggested (Gagne, 1968) that in principle it should be possible to teach any child a relatively advanced skill, as long as it is possible to ensure that the child is taught each of the successively more difficult sub-skills that lead the child from his existing level of competence towards achieving the skill in question. In practice, of course, this may be impossible within the time that is available. In theory, however it may be possible to begin teaching a 3-year-old the skills required by a nuclear physicist, although the chances are that the child will be considerably older than 3 by the time all the preliminary learning needed in order to start understanding nuclear physics has been completed!

The point that virtually all of the intellectual skills acquired after early childhood are essentially the consequences of learning rather than inevitable outcomes of pre-set developmental processes helps to put our ideas about learning and abilities into perspective. There is no inescapable limitation in young children that makes it completely impossible for them to gain mental abilities that are not usually acquired until they are older. There are few rigid limits on what a child can learn. However young and inexperienced the young person, it is rarely wise to leap to the conclusion that gaining some desired skill is impossible for a child of that age: it is always worth trying to help a child to acquire it. It is often the case that much additional knowledge or many intervening skills must be learned before the desired achievements can be made, but that is no excuse for sitting back and leaving things to the imagined effects of mental maturation or the mere progress of time.

3

Mental Activities and Human Learning

In this chapter and the two immediately following ones we examine three particularly important influences on human learning. The first is the kind of mental activity that learners engage in. The second is repetition. The third is building on existing knowledge. The present chapter concentrates on the first of the three influences, learners' mental processing activities.

A truism about learning is that it is something that learners do: neither teachers nor parents can do it for them. The adult who remarks in a tone of pained surprise 'I taught them but they did not learn' is probably thinking that providing the teacher communicates clearly and effectively, learning by pupils will be an inevitable and automatic outcome. But it never is. Learning always necessitates mental activities being undertaken by the individual learner.

However clear and however interesting the material being taught, no learning will take place unless the learner attends to it and engages in the mental activity that is needed in order to make sense of the material. Learning does not always have to be deliberate, but it does always require the engagement of mental processes. The mental activities of individual students form a particularly powerful source of influence on what is actually learned.

The Effects of Mental Processing

The findings of some experimental research show just how important the learner's mental processing activities are (Craik and Lockhart,

1972). The research looks at the consequences of giving instructions to undertake different kinds of mental activities. In one simple experiment, psychologists asked some students to spend one minute looking at a coloured picture. It showed a living-room and was taken from a magazine. Afterwards, everyone was asked to recall the items they had seen in the picture.

Since all the participants had looked at the same picture for exactly the same amount of time, you might expect that there would be little variability in what the different participants recalled. But that is not what happened. In fact, some people retained over ten times as much information as others about the items depicted in the picture. What was the cause of this huge difference in the amount that different people learned? As we have already seen, the reason cannot lie in conditions of presenting the information or in the time that was available, since these factors were identical for all the students.

From a teacher's point of view, it would be especially interesting to know whether these huge differences in learning were caused by events that can be manipulated in the classroom, such as the instructions given to the students, or whether the reasons for the differences were factors that a teacher cannot so readily control, such as the inherent qualities of the people who participated in the experiment. And if the former alternative is correct, exactly what were the causes of the differences in the students' performance? All teachers stand to gain from knowing about factors that can exert an influence on human learning that is strong enough to result in some individuals recalling ten times as much as other people.

So what caused this difference? In fact, at the outset of the experiment (which was devised by Bransford, Nitsch and Franks, 1977), the participants had been divided into four groups. The students who were allocated to two of these groups were told that within the picture up to three very small xs had been inked in. Hence the participants forming one of these groups, Group One, were instructed to look for these xs, by scanning the picture vertically and horizontally. They were also told that they would be asked to say how many xs they had located. Group Two subjects were also informed about the presence of xs, but they were told that the xs would appear on the contours of objects within the picture, therefore they should direct their attention to the contours. In actuality, however, the *x*s did not really exist. The pictures shown to the participants did not contain any inked-in *x*s at all.

There were two further conditions in the experiment. The young students allocated to Group Three were instructed to look at the picture of the living-room and think of actions which they might perform on the objects they saw there. Group Four participants were told that after the picture was taken away they would be required to form a visual image of it. Both these sets of instructions encouraged the students to learn about the contents of the picture.

Subsequently, all the participants were tested to see how much of the information in the picture they had retained in memory. It was discovered that this depended to a considerable extent upon the group to which a person had been allocated. Essentially, the students' recall test scores showed that those participants who were in Groups Three and Four retained very much more information than the other participants. Thus in Groups One and Two only between three and eight items were recalled by each participant, on average. But recall by participants in the third and fourth groups was very much better: the number of items they remembered ranged between 25 and 32 objects.

To say the least, this finding shows that the instructions given to the participants had an enormous effect on what they actually learned. The results of the experiment clearly demonstrate that when young people are exposed to visual information, the extent to which they actually learn from looking at it is by no means determined solely by external factors such as the way in which the information is displayed, or by the amount of time available for study. In the experiment these did not differ at all between the four groups of participants.

What was important were the mental activities that individual participants engaged in as they attended to and perceived the material that was shown to them. When the instructions to a participant specified that the person had to think about the meaningful content of the picture, as in Groups Three and Four, considerable learning resulted. But when the instructions did not require mental processing of the meaning of the picture the participants were look-ing at, as in Groups One and Two, there was much less learning, despite the fact that the participants were attending to identical pictures for the same amount of time.

We might be tempted to conclude that the above findings merely demonstrate that people learn most efficiently when attention is directed to the meaningful aspects of what they see. There is some truth in that suggestion: attending to the most meaningful aspects of what is perceived undoubtedly does contribute to meaningful learning. However, the relationship between what we learn and what we attend to is not quite so simple as that, as the findings of another experiment demonstrate.

In this study (Bower and Karlin, 1974) people looked at pictures of unfamiliar faces. Some of the participants were simply told to note whether each face was male or female. The other participants had to rate the faces according to the degree to which they thought them to be likeable, and also according to judgements about the honesty of the faces. Note that in this study all the participants, and not just some of them, had to attend to the meaning of the materi-als. However, there were differences in the actual kind and amount of mental processing required. Having to rate faces in terms of their likeableness and their honesty almost certainly required more ex-tensive mental processing activity than was needed for simply clas-sifying faces on the basis of their sex.

The main finding of the study was that the participants' memory of the faces (measured by a test of recognition) was considerably better among those individuals who had to rank the faces' person-ality attributes rather than simply deciding on their sex. As in the previous experiment, the conditions of presentation were identical in the two conditions: all the subjects saw exactly the same faces for equivalent periods of time. Therefore, as in the previous experi-ments, the differences in learning must have been caused by the subjects who participated in the two conditions of the experiment undertaking different mental activities.

Presumably, the alternative instructions led to different input processing activities taking place when the unfamiliar faces were perceived. Those students who had to rate the faces' likeableness and honesty had to do more mental work than the other subjects as they inspected the faces, and that led to increased remembering.

Processing Language-based Information

At school, a large proportion of the learning that takes place involves language and the written word. So it is important to discover if, with language-based materials, learners' mental processing activities have similar effects to the ones we have observed with pictorial information. Evidence from further experiments has established that the answer to this question is definitely positive.

In a study conducted by Fergus Craik and Endel Tulving (1975), college students who were enrolled in a course on learning and memory were given booklets containing a number of questions. They were told that each question would ask them about a word that they were going to see. The word was then projected for one second on a screen at the front of the room. After seeing the word, subjects wrote down the answer to the question. For example, a question might ask, 'Does it rhyme with STONE?' If the word that subsequently appeared was BONE the subject would write an affirmative answer. There were three different kinds of question:

1   Some of the questions asked about the meaning of the word that was about to be seen (e.g. 'Is it an animal?').
2   Other questions asked about the sound of the word (e.g. 'Does it rhyme with LEMON?).
3   Questions of the third kind asked about the visual format or *typecase* in which the word was to appear (e.g. 'Is it in capital letters?').

With all three kinds of questions, the correct answer was 'Yes' and 'No' with equal frequency. The student participants each answered 60 questions, 20 of each kind, randomly ordered. Afterwards they were given a surprise test to measure their retention of the 60 words. The test consisted of a list containing 180 words in all. Participants were told that 60 of these items were the ones which they had already seen. Their task was to identify the words that they recognized.

The experimenters wanted to discover whether the different kinds of mental processing activities that participants undertook in order to answer the three kinds of questions would have any influence on the students' retention of the words, as measured by the recognition test. All the words had been displayed for an identical period of time, and exactly the same words were used in the different experimental conditions. (That was achieved by, for example, coupling the same word with a question about its meaning for some participants, and with a question about its sound for others.) So, as in the previous investigations, the cause of any differences in the participants' recognition test performances would have resided in their own mental activities rather than in the conditions under which the materials were presented.

The percentages of words recognized following the different kinds of questions were as follows:

Visual structure (typecase): 26%
Sound (rhyme): 46%
Meaningful category: 72%

In short, the kind of question asked had a large influence upon recognition. As in the other experiments, the findings indicate that the kind of mental processing that occurred when someone perceived a word had a very substantial influence upon the probability of that word subsequently being recognized. As in the previous investigations, there were very substantial differences between the conditions in the amounts of information that the students retained in memory, despite the fact that in each condition of the experiment exactly the same words were displayed for an identical length of time.

Further Investigations of Mental Processing

The above findings are undoubtedly striking, but perhaps we should be more cautious about the way we interpret them. Is it inevitable that they reflect differences in the kind of mental processing that takes place when learners perceive some new information? There could conceivably be alternative explanations. One is that following the different kinds of question, subjects spend different amounts of time actually attending to the word they see.

The findings also raise certain other queries. For example, if, as the results show, questions about the meaning of a word lead to better remembering than other kinds of questions, does it follow that all questions about meanings of items are equally effective, or do some meaningful questions lead to better recall than others?

Another matter of uncertainty is that of the importance of making an effort to learn. In the above experiment the participants were not told to expect a recognition test, but some of them might have guessed that one would follow. It would be interesting to know how the experimental results would have been affected, if at all, had all the participants been making a deliberate effort to learn.

Finally, a factor that could limit the relevance of these findings to the practical concerns of school learning is that in the present experiment there does not seem to have been much incentive for subjects to perform well in the recognition test, whereas in many school tasks there are strong incentives to learn. Is it possible that having more incentive to learn would have influenced the results of the study?

In order to clarify some of these additional issues the authors carried out a number of further experiments, totalling ten in all (Craik and Tulving, 1975). These studies were broadly similar to the one just described, but in most of the further experiments the participants were tested individually rather than in a group. The advantage of doing that is that with individual testing it is possible to exert more precise control over details of the procedure, and subjects' responses can be accurately timed. The period of time for which the words were presented was one-fifth of a second. Participants responded to each question ('Is it a —?') by pressing one of two keys, marked 'YES' and 'NO', as quickly as they could.

One outcome of having more precise experimental control over the presentation and timing of the materials was to accentuate the effects of having different kinds of questions. In all of these additional experiments the participants remembered at least twice as many of the words that were preceded by questions that asked about meanings as the other words: in one study participants retained as much as thirteen times the number of items.

Another finding of the further studies was that the particular form of the meaningful questions was indeed important. This is demonstrated by the findings of an experiment in which the questions that participants were asked concerning the word that was about to appear queried whether or not that word would fit into a given sentence. It was found that when the preceding sentence was relatively complex (e.g. 'The small lady angrily picked up the red —') there was a higher probability that the word that was subsequently shown to the participants would be recognized later than when the sentence was of medium complexity (e.g. 'The ripe — tasted delicious') or was simple (e.g. 'The — is torn').

So, assuming that it is correct to say that the mental processing required for the decision task is related to the complexity of the sentence, these findings confirm that memory for meaningfully perceived items is related to the extensiveness of the mental processing they undertake.

Personal relevance

Adding to the complexity of sentences is not the only way to increase the meaningfulness of tasks. Another important influence resides in the extent to which information has *personal relevance* to the individual. The possibility that those events which have personal importance may be especially well processed was examined by another research group (Rogers, Kuiper and Kirker, 1977). Their study was designed similarly to the ones we have already described, but as an added feature there was a fourth, 'self-reference' condition. In this condition the question that preceded various words asked whether the following briefly displayed item (which was always an adjective, for instance, *happy*, *mean* or *miserable*) was one that described the individual participant. Subsequently, there was a recall test.

As in the experiments reported by Craik and Tulving, it was found in this later study that words which were preceded by questions that asked about their meaning (by enquiring whether the word meant the same as another word) were recalled more frequently than words preceded by questions about their physical structure, by a factor of about three to one. But remembering words preceded by a self-reference question ('Does it describe you?') was even better. The participants' recognition of these items was nearly twice as accurate as it was for words that followed a conventional question about the word's meaning ('Does it mean the same as —?').

A further experiment was designed to examine the possibility that the reason why there was a relationship between learning and the kinds of questions that participants had to answer as they looked at a word was simply due to more time being taken to answer those questions that necessitated taking account of word meanings. In the earliest experiments, it is conceivable that, although all the words were presented for the same amount of time (one second), the length of time for which participants actually attended to them might have varied systematically, according to the form of the prior question. Moreover, it had been noticed by the experimenters that in some of those studies in which subjects were tested individually and their response times to answer the questions were measured, the questions referring to the meanings of items took longer to answer than questions about the words' sounds or visual appearances. Therefore, variations in the sheer amount of time spent in mental processing (rather than in the depth or extensiveness of mental processing that took place) cannot be ruled out as an alternative explanation of the differences in retention.

To clarify this matter a further study was undertaken. In this one the questions that were about aspects of the words other than their meanings were carefully designed to ensure that answering them would take just as long a time as answering questions about the meanings of words. That was achieved by requiring subjects to state whether or not a word had a particular consonant–vowel pattern. For example, the question might ask whether the following item fitted the pattern CCVVC (i.e. consonant, consonant, vowel, vowel, consonant). If the word was, say, BRAIN the correct answer was 'Yes'; if the word was MAKER the answer would be negative. These questions took a relatively long time to answer, the average response time being 1.7 seconds, roughly twice the response time for questions about the meanings of words (e.g. 'Is it a —?').

Despite this, however, the words preceded by questions about their meanings were better remembered. So we can therefore rule out the possibility that the earlier result was due solely to differences in the time taken for the question-answering task. Once again the results support the conclusion that it is indeed the kind of mental processing involved that is the crucial factor.

As we have seen, it is possible to argue that the practical applicability of the findings highlighted in this chapter might be restricted because of the fact that in the experiments, unlike real life, there was no incentive to remember the information. So we need to enquire whether or not one still gets the same results when a deliberate effort is being made to remember the information, and also when learning incentives are present.

Intention to learn

One aspect of the series of experiments conducted by Craik and Tulving was designed to shed light on the effects of having a definite intention to learn. In some of their experiments, but not others, subjects knew in advance that remembering would be tested. Perhaps surprisingly, that seemed to make little or no difference to the results. In other words, the improvements associated with active mental processing were unaffected by whether or not the participants had a clear intention to learn.

Of course, one cannot be entirely sure about a participant's intention to learn unless there are clear incentives involved, and in one experiment the effects of having incentives as such were systematically investigated. Students in one study were told in advance that they would be rewarded with one, three or six cents for every word they recognized correctly. As in the previous experiments, there were different kinds of questions. Thus it was possible to compare the effects on word recognition of (1) the type of task and (2) the level of reward. There was a very clear result. The effects of the varying type of question were similar to those observed in the other experiments, but varying the reward level had no effect at all. This finding indicates that differences in intention to learn or remember were not an important factor in the present series of experiments.

That is not to say that incentives and intentions have no effect in everyday learning. However, the present results do indicate that their effects are indirect ones. Perhaps rewards and incentives affect everyday learning by making it more likely that a person will give a learning task their full attention. But when the level of attention and the kind of mental processing undertaken are largely controlled, as in the present studies, there do not seem to be any additional effects of having incentives to learn.

Mental Processing and Children's Learning

The experiments that have been described in this chapter provide firm evidence that people's active mental processing operations form a powerful and important cause of learning and remembering. Of all the many factors that influence what a person learns, none has a larger influence than the kinds of mental processing activities that are carried out by the learner, deliberately or otherwise, at the time the person is attending to the material or information that is to be learned. Of course, it could be argued that the experimental procedure used in these studies is somewhat artificial: it is not typical of school learning situations, for example. However, there was a very good reason for the researchers using such a procedure, and one that compensated for its apparent artificiality. The reason was that with a procedure like the one adopted in these studies, it has been possible to control or eliminate, or systematically vary, all of the possible influences on performance other than those that take the form of the mental processing activities of the individual learner.

Consequently, it is possible to be far surer than it would otherwise be possible to be concerning the real causes of the differences in remembering. We can therefore state, without any serious doubts, that factors relating to the learners' mental processing activities are responsible for the large and striking effects that were observed.

In all of the above studies the method used for manipulating participants' mental activities involved asking questions concerning words that were about to be seen. However, essentially the same findings are obtained when alternative methods for manipulating participants' mental activities have been adopted, for example, requiring participants to rate items on the basis of the perceived importance or pleasantness, or to detect particular letters, or count syllables (Hyde and Jenkins, 1969). The results of studies using tasks such as these have been very similar to the findings that have been described in this chapter.

Most of the investigations that have been described in the present chapter were conducted with young adults. It can't be taken for granted that we would get the same findings with children. Perhaps active mental processing does not have the same effects on children's learning. We need to confirm that it has the same powerful effects on learning and remembering in children that it has in adults.

In fact, evidence from research investigations shows that the effects of mental processing on learning are just as strong in children as in adults. This can be demonstrated by the findings of other studies. The importance of mental activities in learning by young children is illustrated particularly dramatically in a study by Turnure, Buium and Thurlow (1976). These authors used a procedure that was different from the ones we have described up to now, but as with the previous experiments the intention was to observe the effects of having participants – children in this case – undertake different kinds of mental processing as they were looking at various items, and then assess the extent to which the items were remembered.

The researchers who conducted this investigation introduced the term elaborating to refer to various kinds of mental activities that young learners can perform. In their study, learners were encouraged to act in ways that elaborated the items to be learned, for example, by connecting them or relating them to other materials, or generating an image of them. In real-life learning, as children get older they adopt elaborative strategies increasingly frequently.

Some 5-year-old participants in the present study looked at illustrations, each of which depicted a pair of familiar objects. There were a number of different conditions, but in all of them the same pictures were presented for an identical period of time. So, as in the previous studies, the only factor that differed between the conditions was the mental activity of the participating subjects.

The experimenters were interested in observing the effects of the children's mental activities upon their recall of the objects. In the study, the children were given different kinds of instructions concerning the mental processing activities to be undertaken as they attended to the illustrations which the experimenter showed them.

1 Some of the children were told simply to name the objects they saw.
2 Others were told to make up a sentence that joined together the words denoting each of the two objects. For example, for a picture of a piece of soap and a jacket, a suitable linking sentence would be 'The soap is hiding in the jacket.'
3 Other children used sentences, but rather than making up their own they simply repeated sentences that the experimenter provided for them.
4 Children in yet another experimental condition were asked questions that required them to think about possible relationships of the two objects depicted in the illustration. For example, typical questions were 'What is the soap doing under the jacket?' and 'Why is the soap in the jacket?'

Each child worked through 21 such pairs of pictured objects. Next there followed a surprise memory test, in which one item from each pair was shown and the child was asked to remember the object that went with it. From our knowledge of the experiments previously described we would expect the different tasks given to the children to lead to differences in recall. This did indeed happen in the present study.

What was more remarkable, however, was the sheer size of the variations in remembering between the different conditions of the experiment. The main findings were as follows:

> Those children who were required simply to provide the words for the objects presented to them recalled, on average, only one out of the 21 items.
>
> The children who used sentences to join the words together did somewhat better: those who repeated sentences which the experimenter had provided recalled an average of 3 items, and average recall by the children who made up their own linking sentences was 8 items.
>
> But the child participants who answered questions about each pair of items did even better than that. They recalled, on average, as many as 16 out of the 21 items.

In short, despite the fact that exactly the same items were presented in the different conditions of the experiment for identical periods of time, there were quite enormous differences in what the young children actually learned. As in the other studies, it is clear that the cause of such differences lay in the different mental processing activities demanded by the various tasks. We can note that the procedure in which children were asked questions about the items provided a particularly effective method of helping children to learn. It is one that could readily be adapted for use in school classrooms.

Might it be possible to train young children to use the highly successful interrogative strategy more independently, perhaps by making up questions for themselves? The findings of a study that examined this possibility showed that it could be done by children even as young as 4 years of age. After young children had been taught to ask themselves questions similar to those used in the investigation by Turnure, Buium and Thurlow, it was found that they could remember three times as many items as untrained children. Also, they went on using that useful strategy over a long period of time, without needing to be prompted, and they were able to transfer the strategy to different learning tasks.

Aiding Learning by Structuring Information

Another way in which students' mental activities contribute to learning is through imposing structure or organization on new information. People find it hard to recall information when it takes the form of a large number of separate and unrelated items. Information that is stored in a well-organized manner is generally easier to retrieve from memory when the learner needs it. Consequently, learning and remembering can often be improved by adopting procedures that help learners to form connections between new items that need to be learned and the individual's existing knowledge. A number of research findings that illustrate the practical implications of this will be described in chapter 5, in which the effects of previous knowledge on future learning are explored, but some findings provided in the following section give a preliminary indication of the advantages to be gained from strategies that combine mental activity with the utilization of prior knowledge.

Using a narrative strategy

The influence of a student's organizing activities upon learning and remembering is most clearly illustrated by studies using materials that are presented to the learner in a completely unconnected form. The college students who participated in one experiment (Bower and Clark, 1969) learned twelve lists of words, each containing ten nouns representing concrete items. Some of the subjects studied each list for 90 seconds, and afterwards wrote down the words they could recall. Most participants found this quite easy and were able to remember the majority of the words. After they had worked through all twelve lists, the subjects were asked to recall as many as possible of all the words they had studied, the total being 120 (ten items in each of twelve lists). At this stage those participants who had received no instruction in a learning strategy found it impossible to recall more than a small proportion of the 120 words: average correct recall by these students was less than 20 per cent. The performance of another group of students was very much better. These students had participated under identical conditions, with the same word lists and similar presentation times, but with one difference. They had been instructed to adopt a particular strategy as they studied the lists of words. They were told to try to form a narrative that would connect all ten words in each list.

Some practice lists were provided, so that the students had the opportunity to gain some experience in forming narratives. After a couple of such practice trials all the students found it fairly easy to do so. The following is a typical example of a narrative: it was produced by one of the participants. The ten words that appeared on the list originally presented to the student are shown in italics.

> A *vegetable* can be a useful *instrument* for a *college* student. A *carrot* can be a *nail* for your fence or *basin*. But a *merchant* of the *queen* would *scale* the fence and feed the carrot to a *goat*.

During the experiment those students who had been instructed to use the narrative organizing strategy did not perform any better than the other students at the tests measuring immediate recall of each list. Thus the narrative strategy did not at first appear to have any beneficial effects. However, after all twelve lists had been studied, when the students were asked to recall as many as possible of all the words they had seen, those who had followed the narrative strategy performed very much better than the others. As has been mentioned, the other students recalled less than 20 per cent of the words at this stage. However, the students who had been instructed to use the narrative strategy recalled, on average, more than 90 per cent of the words.

This result demonstrates that a mental strategy that involves learners structuring or organizing the information they perceive can have a huge influence upon what is learned.

Learning activities that make use of the structure of writtten language are particularly effective, but alternative kinds of structuring can also be useful. In general, any procedure that serves to link disconnected items is likely to aid learning. For example, in a number of experiments it has been found that recall of large numbers of separate items is improved when learners are encouraged to sort the items into groups or categories. People are much better at acquiring interrelated bodies of knowledge than remembering unconnected pieces of information. The difficulty of learning unrelated materials is apparent from the difficulty that many students experience in trying to learn items of vocabulary in an unfamiliar foreign language.

Practical Learning Procedures Based on Mental Images

A kind of mental activity that can be particularly effective in some circumstances involves forming visual images of items a person wishes to learn. Mental images often form the basis of memory aids, known as *mnemonics*, which are sometimes recommended by teachers and others for assisting learners to succeed at memory and learning tasks.

People differ in the ease with which they can form visual images (and some normal individuals are incapable of making images at all), but there are some learning tasks in which most people can benefit from using a strategy that requires them to form visual images. In foreign-language acquisition, for example, a mnemonic strategy that involves learners forming images can be very effective for helping students to acquire vocabulary items.

One technique is called the *keyword* method (Raugh and Atkinson, 1975; Pressley, 1977; Kasper, 1983). It provides a way of forming an easily remembered connection between a foreign-language word and its English equivalent. This is achieved by making two links. First, the student learns to link the foreign-language word with the keyword, which is an English word that is easily retained because it sounds similar to the foreign-language word being learned. Secondly, the learner is told to form a visual image in which the item denoted by the foreign word and the object denoted by the keyword are visualized together.

Imagine, for instance, that a student learning Russian wants to remember the word *zvonok* (pronounced, roughly 'zvan-oak'), which means *bell*. Initially, a keyword is formed. In this case a suitable keyword is *oak*. It is quite easy to learn the connection between *zvonok* and the similar-sounding word *oak*. Next, the second link is established, between the keyword (*oak*) and the English equivalent (*bell*) of the foreign word. This is the stage at which an image is formed by the learner. In this example the student might make a strong visual image in which a large bell is seen to be hanging from an oak tree. Having formed these two easily learned links, the student has effectively made a learned connection between the foreign word and its English equivalent.

The method can be used with any language, so long as appropriate keywords can be devised. In selecting keywords, an effort is made to find items which sound as similar as possible to the foreign word and to ensure that each keyword is quite distinct from all the other keywords. Students can devise their own keywords if necessary, but it is usually more practicable for the instructor to provide students with suitable keywords.

The keyword method appears to be somewhat cumbersome: it appears to make vocabulary learning more complicated rather than easier. Nevertheless, it is effective because, like the organizing strategies we have described, it has the effect of changing the learning requirement from the difficult single task of forming a learned link between unrelated words into two much easier tasks.

A number of studies have demonstrated that the technique can be very helpful for students engaged in learning foreign languages. For instance, the college students who participated in one study (Atkinson, 1975) learned forty Russian words on each of three successive days. The learning procedure was one in which a student would hear the Russian word pronounced three times, and simultaneously the English translation of the word would be displayed on a screen. In the keyword condition the keyword would be displayed at the same time. To test learning, the Russian word was pronounced and students were required to type the correct English equivalent. On each of the three days those students who used the keyword technique learned substantially more words than students who followed an otherwise identical learning procedure without the keywords. After the three-day period students were tested again on all 120 words. At this point, those students who used the keyword method correctly recalled 72 per cent of the items, whereas the other subjects recalled only 46 per cent. In order to assess whether this advantage would be maintained over a substantial period of time, the students were tested again six weeks later. On this occasion the students who had used keywords recalled 43 per cent of the words, and the other students recalled 28 per cent. Thus the keyword method was a highly effective aid to students in this arduous and time-consuming aspect of learning a foreign language.

Further investigations have established the effectiveness of the method for students learning other languages. It has been found that when students can choose whether or not to make use of the method they do use it and they continue to do so on a regular basis over lengthy periods of time, measured in months rather than days. For instance, in one study students who had to learn about 700 Russian words over a nine-week period chose for themselves whether or not to use the method throughout the entire period. It was found that as time went on they used the method increasingly frequently. Clearly, the effectiveness of the keyword method is not due simply to its novelty.

Does the technique work for young children? Although very young children are quite good at forming images they find it difficult to transfer information from a verbal form into a visual image and back again. Hence, using the keyword method in the manner described above does present some problems to the very young. However, a modified version of the method has been shown to be effective. The modification involves using pictures in addition to the keywords, eliminating the necessity for the learner to produce, unaided, a spontaneous visual image. Children as young as 6 years of age can use the modified technique. In one study, 6-year-olds recalled eight words out of a list of twelve Spanish words they were taught with the modified keyword method (Pressley, 1977). Children in a control group remembered less than four words, on average.

The keyword method is a flexible device which can be used in a range of situations, not only for acquiring foreign-language words. It has also been successfully adapted to helping children to learn word definitions in English (Levin et al., 1982; Sweeney and Bellezza, 1982). Levin and his co–authors used coloured drawings that depicted the concept to be defined, together with a keyword. For example, with the word pursuade the chosen keyword was *purse*. There was a picture in which some purses were displayed on a shop stand, and two women were depicted, one of whom said, 'Oh, Martha, you should buy that *purse*,' to which the other replied, 'I think you can *persuade* me to buy it.' Underneath, the word and its definition are written, together with the keyword: 'PERSUADE (PURSE) – When you talk someone into doing something.'

Conclusion

What counts, then, is what the learner *does*, mentally. Teaching will be effective for getting children to learn in so far as the teaching encourages learners to engage in the kinds of mental processing activities that result in information being retained in memory or learned. As we shall see later, there are various kinds of learning activities and strategies that maximize the likelihood of effective mental processing activities taking place. At school, those mental activities that produce learning are typically more complicated than the ones described in the present chapter, and they are often deliberately introduced with learning in mind. As children get older they become increasingly adept at using plans and strategies in which their mental activities are organized in ways that are effective for promoting learning.

However, encouraging mental activities is just one of three related and interdependent ways of aiding learning. The second is repetition. This can take the form of rehearsal, or reciting and self-testing, or practising. The third way is to build on existing knowledge. As we have already seen in the present chapter, learning can be aided by various mental activities that make use of what the learner already knows, such as ones that impose structure on unrelated items of new information.

In the next chapter we concentrate on repetition, and show how the combination of activities that ensure extensive mental processing and ones that provide opportunities for repeated exposure to information can aid young people's efforts to learn.

4

Rehearsing and Practising

Most forms of learning depend upon repetition. The kinds of repetition that aid learning take various forms but most fall into one of two categories, *rehearsal* and *practice*. It would be convenient if it took just one single exposure in order for a person to learn, say, the French equivalent of one English word, or remember how to spell a word that is long and difficult, or how to carry out a complicated physical skill. Sadly, however, that is not the case. In the absence of plentiful opportunities for repetition, learners generally make very little progress.

Rehearsing

Rehearsal is a common activity as well as an effective one. It works by giving people repeated exposure to information to be learned. It is a learning *strategy* in the sense of being an organized way in which learners act so as to make learning more likely. In common with other strategies that promote learning, and unlike most of the mental activities that learners engaged in in the experiments described in the previous chapter, it is one that is usually performed only when there is a deliberate intent to learn. Rehearsal is probably the most widespread of all the deliberate strategies used by young students in order to help them acquire knowledge and skills.

Rehearsal is useful in connection with many of the learning tasks that are encountered at school, and most children who have been attending school for several years habitually rehearse when it is appropriate to do so, and thereby gain the benefits it brings. Nevertheless, we are not born possessing the strategy of rehearsing: it does have to be acquired. It is a learned strategy, and one which many young children do not possess.

Although it seems likely that most young schoolchildren could benefit from rehearsing, not all of them do rehearse. Is that just because they have never been taught to do so, and have never discovered the strategy for themselves? Or is it because some school-age children may be too young to get any benefit from rehearsing? Some research has been undertaken in order to explore these issues.

Can young children can be taught to rehearse? If so, does rehearsing bring real advantages to them as learners? If the answers to both those questions are positive, learning how to rehearse might be regarded as a particularly useful way of learning how to learn.

Investigating the Effects of Rehearsal

In order to be able to investigate rehearsal scientifically, psychologists first had to solve the practical problem of finding a way to detect whether an individual is rehearsing or not. We can simply ask a child if he or she is rehearsing, of course, but people's subjective reports about their own mental activities are notoriously unreliable, and that is especially true when the people concerned are young children.

Fortunately, it turns out, rather surprisingly, that it is easier to know if a child is rehearsing or not than to determine whether an adult is rehearsing. It so happens that young children, unlike adults, often move their lips as they rehearse. Because of that, by simply observing a young child's lip movements it is possible gain a fairly accurate indication of the child's rehearsal activities. Researchers have been happy to take advantage of that state of affairs.

In one study of children's rehearsal, John Flavell and his co-researchers (Flavell, Beach and Chinsky, 1966) watched children's lip movements as they looked at common objects that they had been told to remember. Among the older children in the study, who were aged 10 years, as many as seventeen out of the twenty children observed were seen to be moving their lips. But among the youngest children, aged 5, lip movements were seen in only two participants out of twenty.

Predictably enough, it was also found that the older subjects remembered more objects than the younger ones. Of course, it does not necessarily follow that it was the fact that the older children were more likely to rehearse that caused them to remember more. However, the likelihood that more rehearsing did contribute to the better remembering of the older participants received support from another observation in the study, namely that at each age those children who did move their lips recalled more items than those children who did not move their lips.

Taken together, these findings are certainly consistent with the view that rehearsal makes a strong contribution to memory task performance in young children as well as older ones. One way to confirm or disconfirm this would be to discover whether teaching those children who did not rehearse to do so would result in them remembering more. To investigate this, some 6- and 7-year-olds who did not spontaneously rehearse were carefully taught how to do so. These children were simply told to whisper the names of the objects they were looking at until the moment when they were instructed to begin recall. Interestingly, the children did not find it difficult to follow these instructions. Children of this age seem to acquire the strategy of rehearsing fairly easily, if they are properly taught.

What was the outcome of teaching the children to rehearse? Did it improve their remembering? In fact it improved their remembering considerably, to the extent that their success at recalling information now matched the levels achieved by those children of similar age who had rehearsed spontaneously, without requiring any instructions.

Since it is obviously valuable for children at school to be able to rehearse, it is perhaps surprising to find that, even by 10 years of age, not all children do spontaneously rehearse in those classroom situations in which doing so would be definitely advantageous. Why is this so? A possible reason is that, because it is such a widespread and apparently easy-to-use strategy, teachers and other adults take it for granted. They may believe, wrongly as it happens, that all children at school do already know how to rehearse, and that all children appreciate the value of doing so.

Of course, some children are taught how to rehearse by a parent or a teacher, others may acquire the skill through imitating another child rehearsing (perhaps a brother or sister), and some children just discover for themselves that repeating words makes them easier to recall. But there are other young children who fall into none of these categories. For one reason or another they fail to acquire this useful skill. For these pupils, explicit instruction in how to rehearse that is given by the classroom teacher can make a very real contribution towards gaining the learning skills that all students require if they are to do well in the classroom.

Making Use of Rehearsal Skills

It may be easy enough for a child to learn to rehearse, but that does not mean that once the strategy has been acquired a child will make use of rehearsal whenever circumstances arise in which it can be helpful. To gain the maximum advantages of any learning strategy the individual must not only learn how to make effective use of it but must also gain the *habit* of doing so. It also takes time and practice for a child to find out how to use the rehearsal strategy in circumstances that differ from those in which it was initially acquired.

In other words, the young learner has to learn how to apply the strategy of rehearsing. The same is broadly true of many of the habits, activities and procedures that help us to learn. Generally speaking, learning how to be a good learner is not just a matter of acquiring particular techniques and strategies. Teachers need to be equally concerned with helping pupils get into the habit of using and applying newly acquired learning procedures. That is because young and immature individuals do not automatically or spontaneously take full advantage of recently gained skills. Often they need help and encouragement, and they also have to have opportunities to practice an unfamiliar technique or strategy. When young children do gain plenty of experience at using a new learning strategy such as rehearsing it will gradually become a habit, and they will acquire more and more confidence at using it. Even so, when faced with tasks that are new or unfamiliar, many people, adults as well as children (but children especially), are prone to fall back to using those learning procedures that worked in the past, and are tried and tested. That can happen even when it may seem obvious to a more experienced learner that a recently acquired learning strategy would be much more effective.

The Consequences of Rehearsing

Rehearsal can take many forms. The student at school uses rehearsal in order to help retain in memory information that has to be learned or memorized. Typically, sentence-length passages will be rehearsed, rather than single words. Sometimes it will be necessary for a student to memorize materials verbatim or word for word, for example, when a poem or a speech has to be learned. With foreign-language learning it is necessary for single word meanings to be learned. Quite often, however, only the sense or gist of an item of information needs to be learned, so the particular form taken by an effective rehearsal strategy will depend upon the detailed nature of the task.

One interesting study investigating the effects of rehearsal on the acquisition of prose knowledge was published towards the beginning of the twentieth century (Gates, 1917). Gates designed a number of experiments to examine the effects of advising students to rehearse information they were attempting to memorize. These students were learning this information from some prose passages that they had been told to read. Their ages ranged from 9 to 14 years. The passages of prose containing the information to be learned were highly meaningful ones, taking the form of brief biographies. Gates told the students who participated in his study to rehearse the materials by looking away from the passage after reading a portion of it, and reciting the contents to themselves.

One of the findings was that at all ages the participants learned better when a substantial part of their study time was devoted to rehearsal than when the whole period was spent in reading. On the whole, the most successful procedure was to devote about 40 per cent of the total time to reading as such, with the remaining 60 per cent allotted to reciting. In these circumstances students' retention of the biographical information was fairly accurate, and around 30 per cent better, on average, than in the condition in which the students spent the total amount of the study period simply reading.

For the youngest children, who were 9 years old, the advantage of combining reading and reciting over reading alone was greater than that, averaging 36 per cent. For the oldest students, aged around 14 years, there was a smaller advantage of around 18 per cent. But note that even for these students the increase in learning was a substantial one and a very useful one.

The optimal proportion of the study time to be devoted to rehearsal depended upon the age of the learners. For the older children learning was at least as good when as much as 80 per cent of the time was spent rehearsing as when rehearsal occupied 60 per cent of the total study time. But, with the younger subjects, dedicating more than 60 per cent of the time they had available to rehearsing led to decreased learning scores. A likely reason for this age difference is that there is a greater advantage to be gained from rehearsal activities taking the form of reciting information to oneself when the learner finds the material rather difficult than when it is easier (as it would have seemed to the older learners, in comparison with the younger ones).

Self-testing Activities

Related to rehearsing and reciting are a number of broadly similar study activities. These include various kinds of self-testing, in addition to the classroom activity of responding to questions about what is being learned that are posed by the teacher. Studies have been undertaken in order to investigate the effectiveness of these study activities, and other investigations have examined the effectiveness of inserting questions into prose materials that students read. By and large, the research findings are in line with common-sense predictions. Testing does have beneficial effects, their form and magnitude largely depending on the particular circumstances. Similarly, inserting questions into textual materials designed for students to read usually aids learning. It has also been found that questions are more beneficial when they refer to content that a student has just read than when they ask about information in the passage the student is about to read.

In some studies the exact form of the improvements in learning has been found to depend, not surprisingly, upon the type of questions used and their position in the text. An experiment by Duchastel (1982) provides a good example of research into the effects of testing on school learning. American high-school students read a 1,700-word passage containing twelve paragraphs that each described a topic of British history during the reign of Queen Victoria. After reading the prose text some of the students were immediately given a test on the contents of the passage. Some other students, who formed a control or comparison group, spent the equivalent amount of time completing a study habits questionnaire. Two weeks later all the students were tested again, in order to discover how much of the contents of the passage they could still remember.

On this later occasion it was discovered that those participants who had been tested immediately after reading the passage had retained the material much more successfully than the other students. In fact, the tested individuals recalled no less than twice as many items as the subjects who were in the control group. The design of the experiment enabled the researchers to rule out the possibility that the improvement was solely due to some of the participants becoming familiar with particular test questions. This does not seem to have been a crucial factor, since those participants who were given multiple-choice questions in the immediate test and short-answer questions in the long-term test administered two weeks later (or vice versa) performed almost as well as subjects who received the same form of test on both occasions.

Practising and its Consequences

The second, and very different, kind of repetition which plays a vital role in some forms of learning is *practising*. Almost any kind of acquired skill, whether it is a mental skill needed in order to be competent at arithmetic, writing, or playing chess, or skill in the use of equipment, or a sporting skill, or competence at playing a musical instrument, takes practice. Even those individuals who are believed to be especially talented within an area of special ability, irrespective of whether that is mathematics, or chess or a sport, or music, require long periods of training and practice in order to make substantial progress (Ericsson and Charness, 1994; Ericsson et al., 1995; Starkes et al., 1996). And that is just as true in those fields of expertise in which innate talents are widely believed to make an important contribution as it is in respect to other kinds of expertise (Sloboda, Davidson and Howe, 1994; Sloboda et al., 1996; Howe, Davidson and Sloboda, 1998). Typically, the sheer amount of practising necessary to achieve a high level of expertise is considerable.

Consider, for example, the experience of becoming a competent player of a musical instrument. The amount of time that needs to be devoted to practising in order to become a reasonably competent amateur performer at the piano, as assessed by reaching Grade Eight in the examinations that are provided by various musical boards, is very substantial. It averages around 3,500 hours. That is a great deal of time, roughly an hour per day for ten years. Of course, some young instrumentalists get by with less practising than that, but not enormously less (Sloboda et al., 1996).

Although it is commonly believed that there are a few especially talented young players who can forge ahead with hardly any practise at all, in reality that simply is not true. So although some individuals do manage to succeed at the Grade Eight examinations after having practised only 2,500 hours or so rather than 3,500, or in a few instances perhaps as little as 1,500, there seem to be no players at all who reach that standard after, say, only 500 hours spent practising.

Many people cling to the view that practice as such is not really all that important, and that other possible influences such as innate talents are more crucial. However, the facts that research studies have yielded firmly contradict that view. Practising is *very important*. The power of practising is demonstrated by the fact that at least in some areas of skill, such as music, the total amount of practising a person has done is the best single predictor of a young player's progress. And that is despite the fact that the measures of practising that researchers have depended upon have been rather crude ones, often based on individuals' uncertain memories of the amount of practising they did when they were some years younger than at present, and ignoring key influences like the quality of practising altogether. The fact that, despite these defects in the evidence, the amount of practice is nevertheless such a good predictor of progress, suggests that practising is absolutely necessary, and considerably more important than it has generally been perceived as being.

In order to be really effective, practising activities need to be well designed and appropriate for the learner. There is no point in simply repeating an activity that has already been mastered. The practising activities need to concentrate on aspects of a skill in which improvement is needed.

Practising also needs to be deliberate, and concentrated. There are many people who regularly play a round of golf, or games of tennis or badminton, or bridge, year after year, without getting much better. To make a substantial improvement the practising activities need to involve numerous repetitions of those elements of the skill that are defective. Therefore a good piano teacher may tell a pupil to make plenty of repetitions of a sequence of finger movements, or a tennis professional will encourage a young player to make literally hundreds of repetitions of a backhand stroke that is not yet mastered (Ericsson and Charness, 1994). Just playing tunes, or just enjoying a game of tennis, will not be enough to ensure that the highest standards are achieved.

Of course, deliberate practice is not always much fun. It can be boring and may seem unrewarding at the time. It requires a young player to have a healthy capacity to delay gratification, which we observed earlier to be an important ingredient of success as a learner. Young children do not spontaneously choose to spend long hours playing scales on the piano or practising their multiplication tables.

They need plenty of encouragement, given by sympathetic teachers or parents who can inject support and enjoyment into activities that would otherwise seem too lonely, or too arduous or repetitive to sustain a child's interest. That is why whenever one encounters a young child who has made unusual progress at mastering a difficult skill like playing the piano, it almost always turns out that one or more sympathetic adults have made big efforts to provide the needed support and encouragement.

In the series of investigations in which John Sloboda, Jane Davidson and myself looked at the early progress of unusually capable young musicians, we found that virtually all the youngsters had been helped considerably by conscientious and supportive parents. Typically, for example, the parents were present while the young child was practising, and a parent might invent games to make the practice routines more fun. We gained some particularly illuminating responses when we asked the young musicians themselves what would have happened to their practising had the parent ceased to take an interest. Many of the young performers flatly informed us that in that event they would have simply stopped practising (Sloboda and Howe, 1991), that is, they would not have practised at all. And of course, had that happened the consequences would have been disastrous for their musical careers. They would never have made the progress that enabled them to become highly capable while they were still quite young, and the result of that would have been to ruin their chances of achieving the high musical standards that are needed in order for a young person to stand a chances of developing into a professional adult musician.

Conclusion

Repetition, whether it is in the form of rehearsal or self-testing, or whether it takes the form of practising activities, is an absolutely crucial component of learning. It does not always get the attention it deserves, perhaps because rehearsal and practice are seen as rather unglamorous routine activities. But with learning, it is often the ordinary routine background activities that make up a young person's everyday life that are most important, and not the more unusual or exciting events, or the dramatic insights that are more likely to come to other people's attention. The gaining of capabilities and competence is largely a result of steady progress that takes place as a consequence of frequent and regular learning activities, among which repetition, rehearsal and practice play prominent roles.

5

How Existing Knowledge Aids Learning

We do not always notice just how much we depend upon what we know. Yet in the absence of various kinds of knowledge nothing would make any sense. Everyday events would have no meaning. Consider the ordinary experience of understanding the following simple sentence:

The policeman held up his hand and stopped the car.

What does that mean? Before you tell yourself that the meaning is obvious, stop to think what the sentence could mean. The phrase 'held up his hand' could mean that the policemen grasped one of his own hands and simply lifted it up. Alternatively, it might mean that the policemen lifted the hand of a suspect or a prisoner, some undefined 'him'. And what does 'stopped the car' mean? Once again there are various possibilities. For example, it might mean that the policeman, being enormously strong, exerted his strength and literally forced a moving car to stop.

However, the chances are that when you first looked at the sentence you did not think of any of these meanings. Most people who read the sentence for the first time take it for granted that the intended meaning is the conventional one. But there is nothing in the sentence to indicate that any of the alternative meanings I have mentioned is not the intended one, so why should we rule them out?

The answer to that question lies in what we already know about our world and about the ways in which events tend to happen

(Collins and Quillian, 1972). In order to make sense of 'The policeman held up his hand and stopped the car' we refer to our existing knowledge. This usually happens automatically, and we are not aware of what we are doing. But if it was not for the fact that we already possess knowledge in the form of a store of highly organized information the sentence would have little or no meaning for us.

Imagine, for example, that someone who was listening to that sentence came from a part of the world where policemen were never employed for traffic duty. Such a person would derive some meaning from the sentence, assuming that he knew what policemen are, what hands are, and understood what it means to hold something. But that individual would fail to perceive the intended meaning of 'held up his hand'. The person would interpret that phrase as having one of its alternative meanings.

Even for us, had the phrase 'held up his hand' occurred in a context that was different from the one in the above example, we would have interpreted its meaning differently. Consider, for example:

Jack damaged his finger. The doctor held up his hand and examined the injury.

Here we perceive the phrase 'held up his hand' as having an entirely different meaning to the previous one. Similarly, the interpretation of 'stopped the car' that we (automatically) rejected when it was in the sentence about the policeman would be perfectly appropriate if we encountered it in the following sentence:

The charging elephant stopped the car.

An Experiment on Sentence Recall

When we are engaged in the kinds of learning that involve the acquisition of previously unfamiliar knowledge and information we habitually make frequent use of what we already know. We depend very heavily upon our existing knowledge of our world. Consider the following experiment. In one of its conditions, students were asked to listen to a sequence of ten simple statements, like these ones:

The funny man bought a ring.
The bald man read the newspaper.

Afterwards, the students tried to answer questions designed to assess whether they remembered the statements. A typical question asked was, for example, 'Which man read the newspaper?' It was found that, on average, the participants gave only four correct answers out of ten.

Other students listened to longer statements, including the following ones:

The funny man bought a ring that squirted water.
The bald man read the newspaper to look for a hat sale.

As in the previous condition, after listening to ten sentences the students who participated in the study tried to answer questions testing recall of the content. The test questions were identical to the ones given to the other students. But these students did much better than the other ones, answering around seven questions out of ten correctly, on average. In short, the participants who were exposed to the longer sentences recalled almost twice as many items as the other students. That happened despite the fact that the statements they had listened to were considerably longer, which, you may think, should have made them harder to remember rather than easier.

How can that be explained? The experiment had been designed to shed light on the manner in which people make use of their existing knowledge in order to learn from new information (Bransford et al., 1981). If you look back at the longer sentences you will see that they differ from the shorter ones not just in their greater length but in including material that formed links between the sentence contents and information that was already known to the participants. The effect of that was to change the nature of the task quite considerably. With the shorter sentences the relationship between the different items of information in a sentence would appear to a participant to be quite arbitrary, that is, there is no obvious connection between them. But with the longer sentences, the participant is able to see a link between the different sentence elements: they are no longer entirely separate. As a result, the elements of the sentence are now seen to be connected to each other, because each is related to something within the learner's knowledge that forms a link between them.

For example, there is no obvious connection between being bald and reading a newspaper. So the sentence 'The bald man read the newspaper' is made up of two separate ideas. But adding 'to look for a hat sale' to the original sentence provides an understandable *reason* for the bald man to read the newspaper. The extra words direct us to information that lies within our existing knowledge and which provides a justification for the bald man reading the newspaper. So the enlarged sentence now makes sense to us, in a way that was missing when we saw only the shorter previous sentence. And once our existing knowledge is introduced in this manner, we understand the ideas in the sentence as being connected to one another. Consequently, as a learning task, remembering the longer sentences is easier than remembering the shorter ones, because in spite of their extra length the number of entirely separate ideas to be retained is fewer rather than more.

In the experiment, the improved recall of the longer sentences was definitely due to their incorporating information that enabled the different items to be linked to one another by the participants. That the improvement was not due simply to the longer sentences being preferred was confirmed by adding a third condition to the study. In this third condition the sentences were the same length as the longer ones but did not help the participants to form links between the sentence elements. Examples of these sentences are:

The funny man bought the ring that was on sale.
The bald man read the newspaper while drinking coffee.

These sentences were the same length as the ones that the second group of students heard. They were equally meaningful, and probably more interesting than the original short sentences. However, when the participants subsequently tried to answer the questions testing recall of these sentences, their performance was much poorer than in either of the other two conditions of the experiment, with recall averaging only two correct items out of ten. This shows that the beneficial effect of the second of the three kinds of sentences, compared with the first, shorter ones, was undoubtedly achieved by the links that could be made within the sentences in the second group. By introducing their own knowledge the participants were able to form connections between the different parts of a sentence.

Learning and Knowing in Children and Adults

For every individual, learning and remembering are strongly influenced by what that particular person already knows. The effects of a learner's existing knowledge can be sufficiently powerful to offset other powerful influences, such as the large difference in performance at memory tasks that is normally observed when young children are compared with adults. That is demonstrated by the findings of a study in which some 10-year-olds who were good chess-players were allowed ten seconds to look at the pieces on a board forming a chess position (Chi, 1978). Afterwards, they tried to place the chess pieces in the correct places on a blank chessboard. The test was then repeated with adults who knew the rules of chess but were not such good players as the children. All the subjects, children and adults, were also given a separate memory test in which lists of digits were memorized.

When it came to recalling lists of digits, the adults were much better than the 10-year-olds. That finding was not at all unexpected, since adult subjects usually outperform children on simple tasks of learning and remembering. But with the chess pieces, however, the situation was reversed: here the children did much better than the adults. The average numbers of pieces correctly recalled by the children and the adults were respectively 9.3 and 5.9.

Why did the children outperform the adults at this particular task? The reason for the child subjects remembering more items than the adults is simply that the children knew more about chess. At this particular task the children were able to use their existing knowledge about chess in ways that improved performance. For example, they could see that the relationships between the positions of the different pieces were not arbitrary, and therefore they did not need to remember the position of each piece as a separate and isolated item of information.

The age-related differences in learning and remembering that are found in many tasks are due largely, although not entirely, to older people having more knowledge about the material. This was illustrated in a study of memory for words. Initially, 13-year-olds were more successful than 10-year-olds, who in turn did better than 7-year-olds (Ceci and Howe, 1978). However, when the task was slightly changed, to make sure that even the youngest children did clearly understand all the words and also knew how those words were related to some other words that were provided as clues to prompt recall, the age difference completely disappeared. In other words, the effect of ensuring that the youngest participants had all the relevant knowledge about the items that was possessed by the older participants in the experiment was to eradicate completely the usual age difference in degree of success. As a rule, a person of any age will be highly successful in recalling items of new information that are clearly related to an area of interest, even when the person's formal education is limited. So, for example, many thousands of football enthusiasts are highly successful at recalling recent football scores (Morris, Tweedy and Gruneberg, 1985).

Adult–child comparisons when differences in knowledge and strategies are absent

As children get older, they become better at learning and remembering. As we have just seen, one reason for that is simply that older people know more, and consequently are better equipped for taking advantage of the fact that learning increases when people are able to link new information with existing knowledge.

An additional reason for the improved performance of older individuals is that they are better at undertaking appropriate mental activities and strategies. As we saw in chapter 3, a person who mentally processes new information appropriately will retain that information more effectively than someone who does not. Not surprisingly, therefore, age-related differences in learners' activities contribute to differences in performance at learning tasks.

If we carefully devise learning tasks so that both of the above two causes of age-related differences in children's success are eliminated, the age differences in performance disappear. That is, if the performance of younger and older children is compared at a learning task which has been carefully designed to ensure that (a) the older children cannot make use of strategic mental processing activities that are unavailable to the younger participants, and (b) the older children are also prevented from making effective use of their greater knowledge, compared with the younger children, then the usual differences between children of different ages will be much reduced.

Does that actually happen? Consider first an experiment in which the possible benefits of using either good mental strategies or a person's existing knowledge were minimized by using materials that were unusually simple. In this study the participants saw two briefly illuminated lights, one at a time, and separate by several seconds. The participants in the experiment simply had to say whether the second light was brighter or dimmer than the first one. It is clear that this particular memory task, which involved retaining information about the brightness of a light, is not one in which there is much opportunity for subjects to introduce either mental processing strategies or existing knowledge (Belmont, 1978). So was there a reduction in the usual age difference in performance at the task?

In fact, it was discovered that 8-year-old children performed just as well as adults. And in another experiment children as young as 7 years of age were also found to be as successful as adult subjects at another memory task, in which they looked at series of pictures and were subsequently given a recognition test. In that task, two pictures were displayed to the subjects at a time. One of the pictures was new, but the other had been displayed previously, and the participants had to say which one that was.

These findings make it clear that when the task is one in which neither subjects' mental strategies nor their own existing knowledge can make a large contribution, the usual performance differences that favour older people over young children tend to disappear. This is not to say that there are definitely no differences at all in learning and memory between young and older students when the contributions of mental activities and personal knowledge are reduced or eliminated. However, the research findings do strongly suggest that these two influences are responsible for at least a large share of the age-related improvement that is found in many learning and memory tasks.

Using titles to help access relevant knowledge

In the experiments on memory for sentences that were described earlier, the context in which a phrase occurred directed learners towards those parts of their existing knowledge that indicated the most likely meaning for a particular phrase. There are alternative ways of achieving this. For instance, with materials that are ambiguous, difficult or unfamiliar, titles or sub-headings can be useful for guiding a learner towards those elements of her own existing knowledge that are related to the new information. In the absence of such a title, that useful clue is missing. Consequently, when a passage such as the following one is presented without a title, many students have difficulty in making sense of it:

> With hocked gems financing him
> our hero bravely defied all scornful laughter
> that tried to prevent his scheme
> your eyes deceive
> he had said
> an egg
> not a table
> correctly typifies this unexplored planet
> (Dooling and Lachman, 1971, p. 217)

On the other hand, students who *are* provided with a title in advance do not have any trouble understanding the passage. That title, which happens to be 'Christopher Columbus Discovering America', makes it clear to the reader where the information that can help to make sense of the passage is to be located within that reader's body of structured knowledge. Hence, when the title is provided for readers, there is improved comprehension and an increase in learning.

Negative Influences of a Learner's Existing Knowledge

People are – and have to be – very good at making use of what they already know in order to comprehend and learn from new events and experiences. But most people are not so good at remembering when, where or how they gained the knowledge they have come to possess. Fortunately, in most circumstances this does not matter too much. However, on certain occasions it can be important for someone to know how certain items of information they have come to know were first acquired.

Imagine that you spend part of today reading a story that is already somewhat familiar to you. Tomorrow you look at another version of the same story. Later you are asked to identify the particular details that appeared in the version you read today. How well would you do? Students were given such a task in an experimental investigation (Kintsch, 1975). They read passages on topics that were already broadly familiar, such as the biblical story of Joseph and his brothers. A day later their ability to distinguish between the content of the particular passage they had read and their background knowledge of the story was tested. The students found this task extremely difficult, and their performance was poor.

There are certain circumstances in which the errors that people make because of not knowing how certain knowledge was acquired can have unfortunate practical consequences. Think about what happens when someone witnesses an accident or a crime, and afterwards is repeatedly asked to describe what was seen. Understandably, mistakes sometimes occur in the person's remembered descriptions. The problem is that when someone is asked to describe an event for, say, the fifth time, it may be quite impossible for that person to distinguish between his memory of the original event and his memory of his previous recollection of the event. The individual may think that he or she is recalling the actual event, but in fact be retrieving from memory a stored representation that was formed partly by the event itself and partly by subsequent self-reports, in the form of the person's own attempts to recall it.

The effects of that kind of confusion may be fairly innocuous if the earlier attempts at recall are accurate. If they are inaccurate, however, the individual's memory for events may become progressively more flawed, usually without the person being aware of it. Evidence that errors of this kind can and do occur is provided by some research studies conducted by Elizabeth Loftus and her colleagues (e.g. Loftus and Palmer, 1974), investigating the accuracy of eyewitness testimony. These researchers were particularly interested in discovering whether people's memory for happenings such as traffic accidents can be influenced by information that is supplied after the event.

In a typical study some people are shown a film of a traffic accident in which two cars collide. Afterwards they are asked to say how fast the vehicles were moving. However, new information is surreptitiously introduced at this stage by varying the form of the question. Some of the participants are asked how fast the cars were going when they *hit* each other, whereas others are asked to say how fast the cars were going when they *smashed into* each other.

In studies of this kind, it is usually found that the participants' estimates of the cars' speeds are influenced by the form of the questions asked. Those people who are asked about the speed of cars which smashed into each other report a higher speed, on average, than those who are told to report the speed of the cars which hit each other.

Also, the information that was introduced via the questions had some additional effects upon the participants' memories of (as they believed) the original accident. For instance, when the people who had seen the film of the accident were asked whether they saw any broken glass, those individuals who had previously been asked the question which included the word 'smashed' were more likely than the others to respond affirmatively. (In actual fact, there was no broken glass in the film.)

These research findings point to some of the dangers of allowing 'leading' questions, either in legal courts or in any situation in which the aim is to elicit the truth about events which have been witnessed.

Distortions caused by previous knowledge

Another situation in which existing knowledge can sometimes make it more difficult rather than easier to learn new facts occurs when we have to learn something which seems to contradict what we already know. In one study (Ceci, Caves and Howe, 1981) 7-year-olds and 10-year-olds listened to a story in which a variety of well-known characters from television and movies behaved in ways which clashed with the children's knowledge of them. For instance, in the story, the 'Six Million Dollar Man' was told to carry a can of paint, but he could not do so because he was too weak. Children who listened to the story and were tested for recall immediately afterwards had no difficulty in remembering it accurately, however discordant were the actions of the familiar characters with the children's knowledge of them. But if the recall test was delayed by several weeks, recall of the events in the story was not only less accurate but systematically distorted in the direction of the children's prior knowledge of the characters in the story. It appears that when retention of information and events is less than perfect, people make inferences about them, based on prior knowledge. It is important that they often do that without knowing that they are doing so.

At school, it is sometimes necessary for students to acquire new knowledge that appears to contradict what they already know, so it would be useful for both teachers and students to be aware of the distorting influences that existing knowledge can have in such circumstances. On some occasions existing knowledge can make it harder rather than easier to remember facts about other people. That is particularly likely when our personal beliefs, opinions or prejudices are involved. Our existing views about others can impede learning.

Sometimes, beliefs and prejudices can distort perception of what actually happens, but even when the actual perception of events is accurate enough, existing knowledge in the form of ideas and opinions that are central to our beliefs can still exert influences that form further obstacles to learning. This is illustrated by the results of a study in which university students read a 750-word passage that described the life of a woman named Betty (Snyder and Uranowitz, 1978). The students read about various aspects of Betty's life, including her childhood, home life, relationships with her parents and a number of other matters.

One week after the students had read the passage they were given a 36-item multiple-choice test in order to assess how well they had retained the biographical information about Betty. Some of the test questions asked about Betty's relationships with people of both sexes. For instance, one multiple-choice question asked whether Betty occasionally dated men, never went out with men, or went steady. The first choice, that she occasionally dated men, was the correct one. But the students' actual responses to the questions showed that their memory for facts about Betty's life could be strongly influenced by information that was supplied after they had read the passage, if it made contact with their beliefs about people.

In the experiment, after the students had finished reading about Betty, some of them were told that she now lives as a lesbian. Others were informed that her lifestyle is that of a heterosexual person. Despite the fact that, prior to this, all the students had received exactly the same information about the various facts of Betty's life, those participants who were subsequently told that Betty was a lesbian were more likely than the others to recall (incorrectly) that she never went out with men. And conversely, students who were told that she was heterosexual often recalled (equally wrongly) that Betty 'went steady'.

In the process of education it may quite often be necessary for a student to learn ideas and facts that contradict the individual's existing views and preconceptions. Knowing that a learner's prior 'knowledge' (the inverted commas being added here to extend the word's meaning to all that a learner believes to be true, even if it is not in fact true), which normally aids learning and makes it easier for a student to retain new information, can also have a very different effect should alert the teacher to the problems that can sometimes arise.

Advance Organizers for Classroom Learning

Every good teacher knows that students acquire new knowledge most easily when the new information bears some relationship to existing knowledge and is not totally unfamiliar. Information will not be meaningful to a person unless he can relate it to what is already familiar. In everyday life we are constantly using metaphors. Metaphors provide a way of expressing new meanings in terms of highly familiar concepts, such as buildings (for example, 'Is that the foundation for your theory? We need to buttress the theory with solid arguments'), food ('All this article has in it are raw facts, half-baked ideas, and warmed-over theories'), plants ('That's a budding theory. The other idea died on the') or even people ('This theory gave birth to many ideas, but those ideas died off in the Middle Ages') (Lakoff and Johnson, 1980). And as we observed earlier, an appropriate title can have a similarly useful influence, directing the reader to existing knowledge to which the new information can readily be connected.

In school learning, as D. P. Ausubel (1968) has emphasized, how-ever logical and sensible is the material that students are required to learn, if it is not understandable to a particular individual that per-son cannot acquire it in a meaningful fashion. So it is quite possible for learning to be non-meaningful even when the learned informa-tion is inherently meaningful. That is neatly demonstrated by an experience described in an anecdote about a school visit by the educational philosopher John Dewey (Bloom, 1956, p. 29). Dewey, who was observing teaching in a classroom, asked the pupils a ques-tion, 'What would happen if you were to dig an immensely deep hole into the earth?' The students responded with silence and blank stares.

After a pause the teacher muttered something about the question being wrong, and turning to the children he asked, 'What is the state of the centre of the earth?' This time the children all answered immediately with the correct answer, 'Igneous fusion.' It is clear that although the children had learned the literally correct answer, all that they had really acquired was a sequence of words (the answer) to be uttered as a response to another sequence of words (the question). They had not learned anything that had real meaning to them.

That is hardly a satisfactory state of affairs. To ensure that a particular item of knowledge can be meaningfully learned it may be necessary for the teacher to help the student. One way of doing that involves showing learners how whatever is to be acquired can be connected to something that they already know. Alternatively, if that is not possible, a similar result may be achieved by first supplying the learner with knowledge that can perform a kind of bridging function, by forming a connection between the new information and existing knowledge.

Ausubel has suggested that teachers should make devices that he calls *advance organizers* to perform the bridging operation. Essentially, an advance organizer is a piece of information that readily connects to a person's existing knowledge and is also conceptually linked to the new material to be learned. After being exposed to the advance organizer the learner is in a better position to acquire the new, now meaningful information, as a result of knowing how or where to connect the new material to existing knowledge.

Intuitively, the idea of providing advance organizers makes good sense. Indeed, it is widely accepted that in order to teach people about a particular topic it is wise for the teacher to find out what they already know in relation to the topic, and take that existing knowledge as the point of departure for commencing instruction. The precise forms taken by advance organizers will vary according to particular circumstances. For situations where the new material is entirely unfamiliar to the learner, Ausubel recommends devising an organizer which is largely 'expository'. For example, a suitable organizer to precede the teaching of Darwin's theory of evolution to a totally naive student might be a prose passage showing how

Darwin's ideas are related to the learner's general knowledge, and providing a framework summarizing the major ideas in the theory. These can be regarded as forming anchoring concepts that can facilitate learning the details of the theory.

In other circumstances a different kind of organizer might be more appropriate. For example, for a student who needs to gain detailed knowledge of one technique of life-saving and has already learned about a different method, the most effective kind of organizer might be one which directs the learner's attention to some of the similarities and the differences between the two methods. Such an organizer would not in itself provide much new information, but it would help the learner to locate relevant existing knowledge to which the new material can readily be connected.

Research studies designed to evaluate advance organizers have shown that they can be helpful in a range of situations. However, organizers are not easy to devise, and they provide no instant cure for learning problems. A major practical difficulty resides in the fact that, in order to design a maximally effective advance organizer for teaching particular materials to a particular individual, it is necessary to ascertain fairly precisely the present state of the individual's knowledge in relation to the topic. Doing so may not be at all easy. But the idea of using advance organizers remains both appealing and sensible, even if the practical difficulties involved in devising materials that successfully fulfil that function may in some instances be considerable.

Strategies for Learning Unfamiliar Topics

Progressing from a state of ignorance about an area of knowledge to one of expertise and knowledgeability may involve considerably more than simply acquiring a greater amount of information. Very often, learning also involves gaining a deeper understanding of something, or a new perspective on the knowledge content.

Some research by John Bransford and his colleagues (Bransford et al., 1981) provides interesting insights into the ways in which existing knowledge influences learning and also into the manner in which learning contributes to the growth of a person's knowledge. These researchers ask, for example, how a novice at biology might learn about the nature and functions of veins and arteries. What would such a person learn from the statement that arteries, which are thick and elastic, carry blood that is rich in oxygen from the heart, while veins, which are thinner than arteries and more elastic, carry blood that is rich in carbon dioxide back to the heart?

Bransford and his co-researchers point out that what a person will actually learn from reading the above statement will depend very considerably upon that particular individual's previous knowledge. For a student who knows nothing at all of biology and is ignorant of the workings of the heart, the description would appear to be essentially little more than a series of isolated and separate facts. Consequently, for such a student the information in the statement would be very difficult to learn. In order to perceive the statement as being a meaningful one, in which the different facts and ideas are connected to each other, the learner must already possess considerable knowledge about the items and concepts mentioned in the statement, and about their implications.

So from a student's perspective the statement will be meaningful, connected and easy to learn if, and only if, the learner already knows enough about its contents to be able to provide connections between its parts and introduce enough familiar facts and images to make its meanings apparent. Only if the learner can introduce various kinds of pertinent information from his own knowledge base will it be possible for the links between the different parts of the statement to be apparent.

Bransford and his co-authors make a number of suggestions about things that a student might do in order to make the information in the above statement about the heart less arbitrary and more familiar. For example, making an image of an artery in the form of a thick hollow tube might help a student to remember the fact that arteries are thick. Similarly, forming a visual image in which the tube is seen to be suspended by a stretching and contracting elastic band, which causes the tube to move, might help the student to remember that arteries are elastic.

The image might be further embellished, these authors suggest, by including a Valentine's Day depiction of a heart, from which blood is pouring towards the tube, perhaps accompanied by bubbles that are round in shape, like a series of Os, representing oxygen. Forming a composite visual image would be one way – although not the only way and not necessarily the best way – in which a student might make the information in the statement more understandable and familiar, and make it possible to perceive the different parts as being connected or related to one another, as against being simply a collection of entirely separate items of information. In this way the individual is able to make use of existing knowledge as a basis for ideas and images that give meaning and connectedness to the passage as a whole.

Such an approach might be the best possible one for a student whose prior knowledge of the heart is very restricted. However, a student whose knowledge of biology is more advanced might choose to act differently. She might well consider the above image-making activities not only inappropriate but actually misleading. Such images can indeed be misleading, beyond a certain point. On the one hand they would be likely to be helpful for a beginner who lacks the concepts necessary for immediately understanding the actions of veins and arteries. But for a more advanced student, who required a very accurate understanding of the concepts, the kinds of images that have been suggested could certainly be counterproductive. That is because the manner in which they depict the biological processes is oversimplified. And what is more, they introduce a degree of distortion.

That is not an uncommon situation. It is quite often the case that the images, metaphors and analogies which teachers introduce in order to make something that at present is entirely unfamiliar more familiar, and to direct learners to relationships or similarities between new material and what is already known, do introduce some distortions. Consequently, the learner's understanding and learning of the new concepts will be incomplete and inaccurate. Often this is inevitable. If there is a large gap between what is to be learned and what is already known the best that can be hoped for initially is a partial closing of the gap, or some advance towards full understanding. Total mastery may require a number of distinct steps.

The successful learner, when confronted by information that seems to be unfamiliar, is good at searching through his own knowledge base in order to find facts or concepts that can be used to reduce the unfamiliarity of the new data. Making use of effective retrieval skills, the mature student looks for existing knowledge that can be introduced to clarify new facts or form links between them. By doing appropriate mental work, such a learner will be creating for herself the advantages that might otherwise be introduced through the provision of an appropriate advance organizer.

The experiments by Bransford and his co-authors verify the fact that learning can be increased by directing people towards those parts of their prior knowledge that can illuminate the links that exist between new facts that are apparently unrelated to each other. Some further studies build on this research, These studies were designed in order to investigate how learners actively make use of their knowledge in order to learn new materials.

The findings of one experiment, for instance, demonstrate that the extent to which learning is actually improved by students' drawing upon their own existing knowledge partly depends upon the particular kinds of questions that the learners ask themselves. College students were shown sentences such as:

The tall man bought the cracker.

The students were asked to make up a phrase that completed each statement. They either responded to a question concerning what might happen next, or they had to suggest why each type of man might perform the act mentioned in the sentence. It was found that those students who were given the second type of question were able to generate phrases that clarified the significance of the original sentence information more precisely. Also, they recalled the contents more accurately.

Note the similarity between that finding and the results of an experiment that was described in chapter 3, in which some of the participating children were told to answer questions about the relationship between two pictured objects (Turnure, Buium and Thurlow, 1976). It was found that these children recalled more items than children who were given alternative study instructions. In the earlier description of that study, emphasis was placed upon the importance of learners' mental activities. But one might alternatively have noticed that the question-asking activity in that study was effective partly because it provided the young participants with a way of locating information that they already possessed, and which could serve to provide a link or connection between otherwise arbitrary objects.

Further research has established that by 11 years of age some children are already good at judging that stories made from sentences in which the parts are related in a non-arbitrary way (for example, 'The hungry boy had eaten a hamburger') are easier to learn than stories containing sentences in which there is no non-arbitrary relationship between the different elements (for example, 'The hungry boy had taken a nap'). Young people who are aware of that are able to guide their study efforts in accordance with their judgements of task difficulty. The same children are also observed to spend a larger proportion of their time studying those stories they judge to be harder to learn, rather than giving an equal amount of attention to each item.

Another study investigated how 11-year-olds activated their own knowledge in order to clarify information they were attempting to learn. A number of sentences were presented, for example, 'The hungry man got into the car.' The participants in this study were told to add to each sentence a phrase that would help them to remember it. The students who participated in the study had previously been divided into three groups, academically less successful, average and successful, as assessed by teacher ratings and test scores. It was discovered that those children who were rated as being successful at school produced more precise clarifying phrases than the other students. They also recalled more items correctly, when given questions such as 'Which man got into the car?' Interestingly, the successful children recalled most accurately those sentences for which they had added the most precise clarifying phrases. They were also better than the other children at explaining the reasons why precise clarifying phrases led to increased recall.

In short, those students who were most successful at school were young people who tended to be better than the others at making use of their own knowledge when confronted by a learning task containing new and unrelated facts. The successful students were also more aware of their reasons for introducing information from their own existing knowledge.

Can training be effective?

Gaining the ability to make effective use of one's own knowledge is an important aspect of learning how to be a good learner. Can that be taught? Bransford and his colleagues have been interested in trying to devise ways to teach children how to activate those parts of their knowledge that can be effective in clarifying the significance of new information.

It was found that simply explaining how relevant elaborations such as 'The hungry man got into the car and drove to the restaurant' facilitated learning helped young people only to a very limited extent. It was not enough to give training that just consisted of demonstrating to the students the value of using phrases to provide the kind of clarification that is absent when sentences are simply extended (as in 'The hungry man got into the car and drove to work').

There was much more success with training that was carefully designed to ensure that children really understood *why* certain kinds of extensions to sentences made them more memorable. The children were first encouraged to discover for themselves the difficulty of learning arbitrarily related facts. They listened to some arbitrary sentences and were later questioned about them. The poor level of performance at this stage demonstrated to the children that the sentences were difficult to learn. That helped them to be aware of the need for a new and better approach.

Then the children were encouraged to ask themselves questions about the sentences. It was intended that this should help them to become aware that the sentences were indeed arbitrary. For example, with 'The kind man bought the milk' a child might be asked 'Is there any more reason to mention that a kind man bought milk than a tall man, a mean man?'

The next step in the training involved prompting the children to activate information from their own knowledge that would make the sentence element relationships (for example, between the 'kindness' and the 'milk-buying' in 'The kind man bought the milk') seem less arbitrary. For instance, a child might be asked, 'Why might a kind man be buying milk?'

When the child provided reasons which could be introduced to form extensions to a sentence, he was encouraged to ask further questions aimed at evaluating the sentence extensions he had suggested. For example, if a child had suggested 'Because he was thirsty' he might then be asked 'What does this have to do with being kind? Wouldn't a mean man be just as likely to do the same thing?' (Bransford et al., 1981, p. 103).

After they had received training in which they were asked questions like this and were encouraged to generate similar questions for themselves, all the 11-year-olds gained the ability to produce sentence extensions that did succeed in clarifying the initial short sentence by relating the different parts of it to each other, as in 'The kind man bought the milk to give to the hungry child.'

The next step in the study involved testing the effectiveness of this training. In order to do that, the children were given the memory test they had started with, and on which they had originally performed very poorly. This time, instead of correctly answering only one or two questions out of ten, most of the children did perfectly. They also found the task exciting and enjoyable. And when they were asked to provide sentences which would transform short arbitrary sentences into ones that were meaningful and non-arbitrary, over 90 per cent of the elaborations they gave were ones that achieved that function effectively.

These findings demonstrate that it is undoubtedly possible to teach children successful strategies for activating their own knowledge in ways that make new information easier to learn. Of course, some children will need considerable amounts of help in order to become capable of doing this. And as with other acquired strategies that can aid learning, many children need to have a substantial amount of practice before they can gain the habit of regularly making use of their existing knowledge in the most effective ways. Also, teachers and other adults should not expect that a child will immediately transfer or apply their new strategy to novel and different learning situations. As in the case of other procedures that aid learning, spontaneous generalizing and application of the newly acquired strategies to different kinds of circumstances are unlikely to take place until those strategies have become firmly established.

All the same, the capability to make good use of their own existing knowledge with maximum effectiveness when learning new information is an extremely valuable one for young learners, to the extent that time and effort devoted to helping children to learn the necessary skills and strategies is indeed well spent. Quite apart from the obvious improvements in learning that are yielded, possessing such a capability may be helpful whenever a child is engaged in the activity of reading, because a child may find reading considerably more interesting when he or she is actively monitoring and responding to the content rather than passively absorbing it. Bransford and his co-authors point out that as a way to learn material from prose passages, merely rereading the information in a relatively passive manner that does not involve thought about the content is not only inefficient but also boring. But the individual who regularly brings what he already knows to his own learning activities finds the experience much more fruitful and interesting. Good learners, he suggests,

> seem able to place themselves in the role of an explorer or detective who searches for the significance of facts. Learners who fail to do this, who merely reread the sentences in a passage, for example, may find the experience uninteresting and tedious. The processes that underlie effective learning may therefore be related to those that capture students' interest, that motivate them to learn. (Bransford et al., 1981, pp. 107–8)

The Mental Representation of Knowledge

The more informed a teacher is concerning what a student already knows, the better. Existing knowledge provides the starting-point for new school learning. Ideally, a teacher would have a precise and detailed specification of a particular student's knowledge – all the facts, concepts, ideas and skills stored within that person's brain. Such a teacher would be superbly equipped to maximize the student's learning.

Psychologists have long been aware of the potential practical value of having a way of exhaustively describing the knowledge that learners already possess. They have been especially interested in trying to find out how knowledge is actually represented within the mental structures that control human cognition.

Discovering how knowledge is represented in a person's brain may appear to be an easy task, but in reality, however, it is not easy at all. The most elementary questions are difficult to answer. How is the knowledge arranged in the human brain? How many levels of organization are involved? For educators, progress towards a better understanding of the mental structures that underlie knowledge and cognition will ultimately bring great practical benefits.

One approach is to begin by investigating areas of knowledge that are relatively small and limited in scope. In practice, appropriate instances are not too easy to locate, since in most people knowledge about one topic is closely linked to knowledge of other things. However, the authors of one study (Chi and Koeske, 1983) were able to avoid a number of these difficulties by studying a young boy, aged 4, who happened to possess a sizeable body of knowledge about dinosaurs. The boy's knowledge about dinosaurs, while remarkable for a child of his age, was sufficiently limited and circumscribed for it to be possible for the experimenter to ascertain fairly precisely what he did and did not know. The investigation was made easier by the fact that what the boy knew about dinosaurs was relatively separate from and independent of his knowledge about other things.

The authors were particularly interested in how the boy's dinosaur knowledge was structured. Note that the effect on a person of acquiring more information is not simply to increase the size of a person's knowledge. Equally important are organizational changes. These reflect the way information is structured in a person's mind.

Changes in the structure of what a person knows have consequences that affect future learning.

To study the implications of differences in the structuring of knowledge, Chi and Koeske examined two subsets of knowledge within the same boy. They did this by forming one list of dinosaurs which he was well informed about, and a second list of dinosaurs for which his knowledge was much sparser. As they had expected, the boy performed better on learning and memory tasks involving the subset of dinosaurs about which he was more knowledgeable.

A major aim of Chi and Koeske's study was to gain a better understanding of why this was so. They were interested in discovering the precise reasons for people being more successful at those learning tasks in which the materials are highly familiar. In this case they considered two contributing factors: first, knowing more in the simple sense of knowing about a greater number of properties of an item, and second, the way information is organized within the structured knowledge base of an individual. They found that the sheer amount of the boy's knowledge, that is, the number of an item's properties that were familiar to him, did not have a very strong influence on his performance. Organizational and structural factors, on the other hand, had much more powerful effects.

The boy's recall and retention of lists of dinosaurs was found to be strongly influenced by the extent to which the composition of the lists matched the organized structure of his own knowledge. Important factors were the number of links, in the boy's knowledge base, between the different items in lists of dinosaurs, the strength of the linkages and the patterning of the links between the various items.

There is a clear practical implication of this finding. It is that, in order to maximize effective classroom learning, we should have a full understanding of how a student's knowledge is organized and interrelated. Just knowing what the learner knows about individual facts and concepts is not enough.

Hierarchical representation of items and their properties

A second approach that aims to shed light on the manner in which knowledge is represented starts by suggesting a straightforward way in which related facts and concepts could conceivably be represented. If it turns out that a person's knowledge is actually organized in that way, we should be able to make certain predictions. For example, tasks in which we need to bring together items of information that are adjacent within the structure of a person's knowledge should be performed more easily or more accurately than tasks involving the bringing together of more distant items.

So if the predictions that we make on the assumption that our guesses about the way in which knowledge is represented in a learner's memory structure prove to be accurate, this would indicate that our hypothesized structure corresponds with the actual organization that exists. Conversely, wrong predictions would indicate that the suggested representation of knowledge does not correspond with reality.

Such an approach was followed by Collins and Quillian (1969). They believed that some kinds of information about objects and their properties might be represented hierarchically on a number of separate levels. Level One, the top level, represents a very broad class of objects, 'animals', and lists attributes of animals in general. On the lower levels there are successively smaller classes of items, together with their attributes, the classes at each of the levels being sub-categories of those at the level above. So one sub-category of animals would be 'mammals' and a sub-sub-category would be 'the cat family'.

Collins and Quillian asked some students to perform a number of tasks that were designed to show whether or not such a representation bears any resemblance to the way in which information about these items and their attributes is actually represented in the organization of a person's body of knowledge. If their suggestion about hierarchical representation of objects and their properties really does correspond with how a person's knowledge is structured, it ought to follow that tasks which involve a person bringing together items of information that are depicted as being widely separated will take longer to perform than tasks that involve items of information that are adjacent to each other.

For example, the question 'Is a canary yellow?' can be answered from information that is all stored more or less together, at one mode, according to Collins and Quillian. However, to answer 'Does a canary have gills?' it would be necessary (if knowledge is structured in the hierarchical manner they suggest) to transmit information between nodes that are widely separated, in order to bring together all the information that is needed to answer the question. Hence it is possible to get some idea of how accurately their hierarchical model depicts how knowledge is actually represented in human memory by seeing whether the relative times that students take to respond to various questions correspond with predictions generated by the hierarchical model. Students were asked to decide on the truth or falsity of various propositions, and the time taken to respond was recorded. The propositions included the following:

> An ostrich can move around
> A canary has gills
> Salmon is edible
> A shark has wings
> A fish can swim

If the hierarchical model of Collins and Quillian does provide an accurate representation of the organization of a person's knowledge, the time that is taken to decide about the truth of, say, 'Salmon is edible' will be shorter than the time necessary for deciding that, for instance, 'A shark has wings.' In order to decide about the latter proposition it is necessary to retrieve and combine information from separate points that are at different levels. With the first statement this is not necessary. The authors predicted that the response time for verifying a statement would be directly related to the number of levels between which information would need to be transferred.

The findings were broadly in line with the predictions. Thus the average time to respond to a question based on information that is all represented at the same level (for example, 'A canary can sing') was shorter than the time to respond to a question requiring information stored at adjacent levels (for example, 'A canary can fly'). This in turn was shorter than the time needed for questions using information from non-adjacent levels (for example, 'A canary has skin').

These results provide a degree of support for the view that the manner in which objects and their attributes were depicted by Collins and Quillian, involving hierarchical organization into broad classes and narrower sub-categories, does bear a resemblance to the manner in which information is actually represented in the knowledge stores of real people.

This research is undoubtedly ingenious, and it provides an interesting way of trying to make progress towards the highly desirable goal of discovering how knowledge is represented within human cognitive structures. However, various findings from later investigations have not been in accord with the predictions about relative response times that are generated by depictions in which knowledge organization is seen as being hierarchical and involving a number of separate but linked levels. For example, a multi-level hierarchical representation would generate the prediction that when questions are asked about items of information that are said to be stored at the same level within a semantic hierarchy (for example, 'Is a cantaloupe a melon?') they would be answered more quickly than questions involving information at different levels (for example, 'Is a cantaloupe a fruit?'). In fact, experimental research has established that that is by no means always the case (Rips, Shoben and Smith, 1973).

Also, a study by Carol Conrad (1972) showed that varying the form of the assertions that subjects were required to verify led to differences in the pattern of response times that would not have been expected if the structures as depicted by Collins and Quillian accurately represent reality. They asked people to decide on the truth of lists of statements in which the sentence subject was retained but the predicate varied, as in:

A canary has skin
A canary can fly

Conrad, on the other hand, presented sequences of sentences in which the subject varied, as in:

An animal has skin
A bird has skin

That ought to make no difference to the response times, according to the Collins and Quillian account. But it does make a difference, a fact which provides evidence of deficiencies in the organizational structures suggested by Collins and Quillian.

Almost certainly, the manner in which these authors originally described the representation of knowledge in the human mind is too simple to be accurate. In reality, the way in which people's knowledge is structured is more complex than they envisage. To make matters even more complicated, the precise manner in which knowledge is structured partly depends upon factors that are unique to each individual. Nevertheless, that which a person knows must be arranged, patterned and organized in some describable manner, and in principle it ought to be possible for psychologists to be able to describe how that is done. The approach of Collins and Quillian can be seen as an imaginative attempt to move in that direction. For teachers, the practical value of being able to make accurate descriptions of how a particular child's knowledge is actually represented will be enormous.

Scripts and schemas

The third and final approach that we shall consider gives attention to the representation of themes and sequences of events. Words such as *schema* and *script* frequently occur in descriptions of this research, which had its roots in some early investigations of people's memory for stories, undertaken in the 1920s by F. C. Bartlett. He defined a schema as 'an active organization of past reactions, or of past experiences, which must always be supposed to be operating in any well-adapted response' (Bartlett, 1932, p. 201).

Bartlett, who was one of the first psychologists to advance the view that knowledge was represented in the form of unconscious mental structures, considered that following exposure to many events and items of information the brain retains some kind of 'generic cognitive representation' or *memory schema*. Such a schema contains stored information concerning the essential structures or elements that a large number of informational inputs have in common. Some modern psychologists prefer to use the word *script*, but with essentially the same meaning. Thus,

> As an economy measure in the storage of episodes, when enough of them are alike they are remembered in terms of a standardized, generalized episode which we will call a script. (Schank and Abelson, 1977, p. 19)

When an individual is exposed to information that is new and unfamiliar he is said to make an 'effort after meaning', attempting to relate the new material to the contents of an existing schema. So far as learning is concerned, that is very useful, because there is strong evidence that information related to a schema or script (or 'theme') is likely to be better remembered than information that is not related to any schema of the learner.

In recent years considerable emphasis has been given to the importance of schemas or scripts for learning and understanding. They provide frames of reference that help us to comprehend and remember events we experience. They serve as frameworks of organized knowledge to which new events can be connected. For an example, look at this little story:

> John went to a restaurant. He asked the waitress for *coq au vin*. He paid the bill and left.

Although it is short, the story is quite meaningful. The reader has a fair idea of what happened. But notice how much it does *not* say. For instance, there is no mention of whether John found a free table in the restaurant or if he sat down to eat. The account does not even specify that John ate from a plate or used a knife and fork.

Nevertheless we, the readers, assume that these events probably did occur. Why? We do so because we make inferences on the basis of our stored knowledge about the kinds of things that normally happen when a person goes for a meal in a restaurant. Within our store of knowledge about the world we inhabit there exists something that we might call a 'going for a meal in a restaurant script (or schema)', representing the bare bones of such events, the essential structure that is common to most actual visits by individuals to particular restaurants.

Someone who has been to restaurants on a number of occasions will have acquired a schema (or script) that contains information about the likely sequence of events: we know what it is like to have a meal in a restaurant. And because we possess an appropriate schema, we can fill the gaps in the account of John's visit to the restaurant. It is a meaningful account, but only by virtue of the fact that we already have the necessary schema or script, enabling us to fill in the background context. Therefore, we do not need to be told all the small details when we are reading an account of a person visiting a restaurant.

Knowledge in the form of scripts also enables people to understand instructions and follow procedures that would otherwise be incomprehensible. Consequently, we can catch trains from unfamiliar stations, or visit a theatre for the first time, without having to learn all the appropriate procedures from scratch. In each of these situations we know, at least in a general way, how these things are done (Schank and Abelson, 1977). We do not have to be given precise and detailed instructions on each occasion we visit a theatre or use a railway station.

For school learning, it is especially important to realize that schema-related information is relatively easy to comprehend and learn. However, a young child who *lacks* appropriate schemas will find a story or an account of events hard to remember. In children, possession of a schema does not guarantee that the stored knowledge in it will actually be used effectively for aiding learning, but it has been shown that 7-year-olds who do not initially make good use of that knowledge can quite easily be trained to do so. These researchers found that older children and college students used their knowledge about conventional forms of story structures to aid retention of new stories that were presented in a scrambled form. The younger children were also able to do so, but only after a brief training procedure.

Even the most ordinary actions are better remembered when they form part of a schema-related sequence. A study by Brewer and Dupree (1983) showed that simple activities such as walking into a room, removing clothes, picking up objects and moving them around, and looking at a watch, were much more often recalled when they formed part of a 'plan' schema (for example, opening a drawer in order to take out a stapler) than when they did not (for example, simply opening a drawer for no apparent reason). The implication for school learning is that the likelihood of a student retaining some information about events and activities can be usefully increased by placing the information within a context about which the young person already possesses organized knowledge in the form of a schema.

6

— Intelligence and Human Abilities —

Even the youngest children vary considerably in their mental abilities. Some appear smarter or cleverer than others, and seem 'brighter' and more astute, able to grasp ideas more quickly. These tend to be the children who make most progress at school. Consequently, it is widely agreed that there exists a trait of general intelligence, and that a child's intelligence level, in relation to the intelligence of others, is a major ingredient of school success. And if a child's intelligence level is important, it makes sense to obtain measurements or assessments of children's intelligence.

So from around the beginning of the twentieth century considerable resources have been directed towards devising and improving tests of intelligence. Intelligence tests can be a convenient means of gaining a broad indication of a person's performance at a range of tasks requiring intellectual skills. A single summary measure of people's level of performance at such tests, the *Intelligence Quotient* or *IQ*, has been widely used as a broad indication of an individual's intelligence. The IQ score of 100 is allocated to individuals whose performance level at the test is average, and the extent to which a person's score departs from that provides an overall assessment of the degree to which that individual's intelligence is higher or lower than average.

Intelligence Testing in Practice

A child's IQ score is a moderately good predictor of that young person's future progress at school. That is hardly surprising, because when the earliest intelligence tests were devised, by a French psychologist named Alfred Binet, the main reason for producing a test was to provide a way to identify those children whose mental capabilities were too limited for them to thrive in an ordinary classroom, and who therefore needed to be taught separately in a special school. At that time, when Binet was looking for suitable test questions he asked teachers to provide problems and tasks that they thought would draw upon the mental skills necessary for school success. So right from the beginning, the contents of intelligence tests have been based on school-related skills and capabilities (Howe, 1997).

As intelligence testing became increasingly common towards the middle of the twentieth century, considerable importance began to be attached to IQ scores and other measures of intelligence test performance. It was widely taken for granted that a child's IQ was absolutely crucial. There were three related reasons for that belief:

First, IQs were seen as excellent predictors of success at school achievements and success at other accomplishments that were related to school performance.

Second, a person's IQ was seen as being an inherent quality of that individual, and to a considerable extent unchangeable.

Thirdly, it was believed that an IQ score was not merely an assessment of someone's level of performance at a test, but an indicator of an underlying trait of intelligence that was the cause of intelligent behaviour. In other words, people were seen as differing in the degree to which they possessed an underlying quality of intelligence, and a child's intelligence test score reflected this underlying quality. According to this view, every person's brain possesses, to varying degrees, some specific capacity for intelligence, and it is that which makes them intelligent and provides the reason for people differing in their mental capabilities.

Up to a point, intelligence testing has been a useful activity, and it has provided a practical means of quickly obtaining a broad indication of individuals' capabilities. Within education, this has on occasion been helpful. More problematically, however, a child's IQ score has sometimes been taken to provide a firm indication of that child's future potential. It has been assumed that a young person whose IQ score is low will simply be incapable of certain accomplishments, and a child's low IQ has been used to justify denying that child access to educational opportunities. Such a practice was particularly common at the time when the 'Eleven Plus' examination was widely used in Britain.

Another problematic feature of intelligence tests is that they do not, strictly speaking, provide measures of intelligence in the sense that measures of other variables are possible. Many scientific concepts are defined in precise terms which specify the operations necessary for objectively measuring them. Accordingly, for instance, in order to discover how to measure temperature in degrees centigrade or distance in metres one simply needs to know how these terms are defined. But that is not possible with the psychological concept of intelligence. It has not proved possible to define intelligence in terms that show precisely how it is to be measured. Definitions vary. Most psychologists who have used the word would agree that it refers to a person's intellectual abilities, but disagreements crowd in as soon as one starts to be more precise. The statement that 'intelligence is what intelligence tests measure' is accurate in its way, and it warns us not to expect too much guidance from any definition of intelligence.

How Useful are Intelligence Test Scores as Practical Predictors?

If intelligence test scores are to be used as a basis for making any kind of prediction, let alone ones that may contribute to children being selected to receive certain opportunities or to be excluded from having access, it is essential to be sure that such test scores really are good predictors. So just how effective are such tests for yielding scores that form a basis for making valid predictions about a child's future success?

The short answer is, not very effective at all. A substantial amount of research has been conducted in order to ascertain the extent to which differences between individuals in their success at meeting various kinds of challenges is predicted by differences in test scores. The method used to gain this information is to calculate the correlation – a measure of the degree of relationship – between individuals' test scores and their actual performance in some area of accomplishment. A correlation of zero indicates that these two variables are unrelated, and a correlation of plus one indicates that the two are perfectly related. So, for example, if the ranking of a group of children for their intelligence test scores at the age of 8 was exactly the same as their ranking on A-level scores at 18, the correlation value would be one. Correlations between zero and one indicate that there is a relationship, but an imperfect one.

A useful indication of the actual degree of relationship is obtained by squaring the value of the correlation. Thus with a correlation of, say, 0.6, the square of that, which is 0.36, indicates the percentage of the variation in people's performance levels at one measure that is attributable to variability on the other measure.

So, for example, were we to discover that there was a correlation of 0.40 between children's intelligence test scores and assessments of their job success some years later, that would mean that 16 per cent (i.e. 0.40 squared) of their variability in job success could be attributed to their variability in intelligence test scores. Consequently, knowing about their intelligence test scores enables one to predict 16 per cent of the differences between individuals in their job success assessments.

Note that because it is the square of the correlation rather than the correlation as such that is the important figure, only when correlations are fairly close to one are they indicative of a state of affairs in which accurate practical predictions are possible. So for example, with a correlation between two variables of 0.8, it would be reasonable to assert that differences on one measure will predict differences on the other, accounting for 64 per cent of those differences. Here it is clear that the scores on one measure will be very useful for predicting performance on the other. But with a correlation of, say, 0.3, the practical value of that correlation for making predictions about individuals is much more dubious. The square of 0.3 is just 0.09, which implies that only 9 per cent of the differences between individuals at one of the variables is predicted by their scores on the other one. Hence, as a practical aid to making predictions about individuals, the value of knowing one score will be close to nil. Knowing one score will make only a very slight improvement over chance to estimating the other score. Other influences will account for over 90 per cent of the differences between individuals.

What this means in practice is that if a test score is to provide a valid basis for making helpful predictions about individuals, it is necessary that the correlation between the test scores and whatever other measure it is that the test scores are being used to predict must be fairly high. A correlation of 0.7 means that the test score is accounting for just half (or 0.7 squared, which is, to be precise, 0.49 of the variability). With correlations lower than that, only a minor portion of the variability is accounted for. And when correlations are less than 0.5, only a quarter at most of the variability in performance on one measure is attributable to variations in scores on the other, in which event the practical value of using test scores as a basis for prediction about individuals is minimal. (Nevertheless, correlations of this magnitude may be useful for making predictive statements about the average performance about large *groups* of individuals.) So far as making predictions about individuals is concerned, when the correlations are appreciably less than around 0.5, the test scores will not be a valid basis for practical predictions.

So what *are* the magnitudes of the correlations actually observed when researchers calculate the degree of relationship between individuals' intelligence test scores and indicators of the same individuals' success or progress in gaining capabilities that matter in real life? The observed correlations have varied from study to study, even when the same indicator is being related to scores at the same test, but the size of the correlations is rarely more than 0.6 and quite often as low as 0.3 or even less. One investigator who had surveyed the various research findings concluded that the true average correlations between intelligence and job performance was certainly no higher than 0.4, and probably nearer 0.2 (McClelland, 1973). Whichever of those figures one accepts, the test scores would have accounted for only a small proportion of variability in real life success. Howard Gardner (1995) has reached a similar conclusion: he estimates that the vast majority of the observed predictions between test scores and the educational, vocational and other practical outcomes that they might be expected to predict actually account for less than 20 per cent of the variability between individuals. In other words, 80 per cent at the very least of the important contributing influences to variability are not assessed at all by giving a person an intelligence test.

These findings suggest that, while intelligence tests may not be entirely useless for making the kinds of predictions that would justify their use for selection purposes, the predictive value of the tests is, at best, very limited. That conclusion gains support from other kinds of evidence. For example, some research has shown that people with lower IQ scores are often more successful at various kinds of achievement that depend upon mental ability than people with higher IQ scores. The author of one study, James Flynn (1991), examined data on people from China who had emigrated to the United States in the period immediately following World War II. Flynn discovered that the average IQs of these individuals was below the average for white Americans, and yet their actual achievements were considerably above average. More than half of these immigrants gained professional job status, for example, almost twice the proportion in the wider American population.

The conclusion that influences which are not reflected at all in a person's IQ score are responsible for most of the differences between people in their actual performance at problems requiring mental abilities is also supported by the findings of other research. For example, studies in which people's capabilities were assessed at cognitively demanding problems requiring difficult arithmetic skills (Scribner, 1984), managerial abilities and the capacity to undertake very complex calculations (Ceci and Liker, 1986) have all shown that the extent to which people succeed at these tasks may be unrelated to their intelligence test scores.

Finally, it is worth pointing out that, even when intelligence test scores turn out to be reasonably good predictors of future success, it does not necessarily follow that such success is a direct consequence of a person having the mental skills that lead to good test performance. The reason for saying that is illuminated by some findings of research initiated in California by Lewis Terman. He and his colleagues selected a large sample of children on the basis of high intelligence test scores, and followed their progress throughout their lives. Sure enough, the high-scoring children tended to have successful careers. However, they also tended to come from fairly wealthy or cultured homes, and it was later discovered that, had the children been selected solely on the basis of knowledge of their family backgrounds, without taking any account at all of intelligence test scores, equally valid predictions could have been made about their future success. It appears that the test scores were useful predictors at least partly because they served as markers or indicators of the kinds of family backgrounds that produced children who would become successful adults (Ceci, 1990; Howe, 1997).

Is Intelligence Largely Unchangeable?

The second widespread belief about the variety of intelligence is that it is largely unchangeable. It is seen as a fixed quality of individuals. It is important to ascertain whether or not that belief is soundly based, because people draw important practical implications from it. Obviously, if intelligence is largely unchangeable, there is no point in making enormous efforts to alter it, and a certain amount of fatalism about the likely prospects of children whose intelligence test scores are low would appear to be justified. According to the authors of an influential American book, *The Bell Curve* (Herrnstein and Murray, 1994), intelligence cannot be changed. Consequently, these authors believe, society is being swamped by large numbers of unintelligent children. These children are, we are warned, doomed to become members of a vast underclass made up of unintelligent adults. Such individuals are, according to this alarmist account, largely unemployable and to a considerable extent incapable of enjoying constructive or useful lives.

That nightmare scenario revolves around the assumption that intelligence is to a considerable extent unchangeable. If that assumption is wrong, the pessimism is unjustified. In that event there will be every justification for doing all that is possible to help those with low scores to extend their mental abilities. And as it happens, contrary to the belief that a child's intelligence cannot be altered, there is plenty of strong evidence conclusively demonstrating that it can indeed be increased, sometimes very considerably. Findings from a number of different sources all support that conclusion (see Howe, 1997, 1998).

1   First, for example, there are the findings of a variety of investigations that have examined the outcomes of adoption. The results show that an adopted child's IQ can be as much as 20 points higher than would be expected if it were true that intelligence was unchangeable and tied to the intelligence of the biological parents.

2   In addition, results pointing to the changeability of intelligence have been obtained from a large number of intervention studies evaluating programmes of early education that were designed to provide educational experiences aimed at children from disadvantaged or deprived environments. The findings of these evaluations provide further evidence of substantial improvements in intelligence.

3   Further evidence of substantial increases comes from investigations that have examined how average test scores have changed over the generations. These changes are usually hidden from view, because when tests are updated or modified it is customary for the average scores to be artificially recalibrated, in order to ensure that the average person's IQ remains at 100. However, when the real scores (i.e. the scores that would have been obtained had the calibration not been done) are examined, a very different picture emerges. It then becomes clear that there have been substantial improvements in average test scores from one generation to another. This has happened in a considerable number of different nations. For example, in France between 1949 and 1974 there was an average gain in IQ scores of as much as 20 points, presumably reflecting a variety of positive influences, including improved education, greater prosperity and better nutrition (Flynn, 1987).

4   Substantial additional evidence of the changeability of intelligence has emerged from studies examining the effects of variations in the amount and quality of schooling children receive (Howe, 1997). In one study it was found that the intelligence of boys who dropped out of school early decreased by nearly two points per year, compared with that of comparable pupils who stayed at school. In other studies, conducted in nations in which the age at which a child starts school can vary by almost a year according to whether or not the child's birthday falls before a certain date, it was found that the intelligence of those 8-year-olds who had received the largest amount of schooling was closer to that of the least schooled 10-year-olds than that of the least schooled children of their own age.

Findings from these and other sources provide overwhelming evidence that intelligence is indeed highly changeable. Even so, some writers have refused to accept that conclusion. They have argued, for instance, that certain of the improvements produced by educational intervention programmes have faded away after some years. They have also noted that such programmes have not always led to major increases. In addition, some writers have observed, quite correctly, that by and large, in the majority of individuals intelligence test scores do stay moderately stable from one year to the next.

But these objections are far from being convincing. Consider first the objection that some improvements tend to fade away. Such fading does indeed occur in some circumstances, but that is just what one would expect, assuming that intelligence is indeed changeable. Fading of improved intelligence scores happens for exactly the same reasons that most acquired skills tend to fade when there is a lack of opportunities to practise them.

Similarly, the fact that not all intervention programmes designed to increase children's IQs have had large effects is an inevitable consequence of the fact that intervention programmes have often been under-resourced, poorly staffed and too small in scale to make a real difference. It is known that large amounts of time and effort, often involving thousands of hours, are needed to enable young people to become skilled and competent in areas of accomplishment such as music (Sloboda et al., 1996). The fact that some inter-ventional programmes have been very successful in raising IQ de-spite the fact that their duration has been much shorter than that needed to produce high levels of competence in much narrower skill areas, including music, provides a firm demonstration of the alterability of IQ scores.

The basis of the third objection, the fact that IQ levels tend to be stable in individuals, is not a genuine reason for claiming that they cannot be changed. It has no genuine bearing on the matter. Most people's home addresses and telephone numbers stay the same from one year to the next, but nobody has suggested that that means people are incapable of moving house! The reason why people tend to remain at the same address is that their circumstances remain unaltered. But when there is a specific reason for someone's address to change, it does so, and exactly the same is true of IQ scores.

Intelligence as a Fundamental Quality of the Mind

According to the third and last of the common beliefs about intel-ligence that were described at the beginning of the chapter, intelli-gence is a fundamental underlying quality of people's minds: it is what makes people intelligent. In other words, the reason why some people are more intelligent than others is that they possess an espe-cially powerful version of an underlying intelligence. That view of intelligence as a fundamental quality or faculty of the mind has been vigorously promoted since the beginning of the twentieth century, originally by a psychologist named Charles Spearman.

In fact, however, that view is too simple to be true. Intelligence is not a single trait, and the idea that there is a single or unitary cause of differences between people in their levels of intelligence fails to take into account the immense complexity of the human brain. To say there is one particular reason for someone being more intelli-gent than another person is no more realistic than saying that there is one reason why today is sunny, or one reason why a nation's economy is in good or poor shape, or one reason why your factory is more productive than mine or why my car goes faster than yours.

In all these cases, we take it for granted that these indications of performance – the weather, the health of an economy, the productivity of a factory, the speed of a car – are the outcomes of large numbers of complicated factors. We appreciate that with any complex system, numerous interacting factors determine their performance levels. So if I was to assert that the reason why my car goes particularly fast is that somewhere in its innards there is a particularly good 'speed module', I would rightly be accused of being simple-minded. The velocity of vehicles is not determined in that way: the true causes are far more complex.

There is a similar case with intelligence and the human brain. A statement about someone's level of intelligence is a statement about their performance level. It describes the outcome of the person's mental activities, but it is not a statement about the reasons for or causes of being intelligent. To say that high intelligence is the cause of doing well at an intelligence test is not a genuine explanation, because it does not identify the actual reasons why a person does well. Such a statement is rather like asserting that a vehicle goes fast because it possesses speed, with the implication that there is some underlying quality of speed that causes a car to travel fast.

In short, then, the word 'intelligence' refers to the state of being intelligent. It is a concept that describes or identifies that state of affairs. But, in common with other descriptive concepts, such as 'speed' or 'productivity', it does not explain that state of affairs. It does not tell us *why* someone is more or less intelligent. The real causes of that are numerous and complicated, and doubtless vary from one individual to another, just as the causes of a sunny day or an improvement in a nation's economic health are numerous and highly complicated.

Intelligence and Human Learning

It is widely believed that intelligence level is a good indication of ability to learn. We assume that an intelligent person must be effective at learning. Indeed, certain definitions of intelligence state this explicitly. In fact, however, the evidence is that correlations between measures of intelligence and measures of learning are very low: knowing a person's score on an intelligence test does not lead to accurate predictions of that person's performance on a learning task.

There are a number of reasons for this. One is that a person who is good at one kind of learning may have less success at other forms of learning. Playing football and programming computers are two skills that depend heavily on learning, but being good at one of them does not lead to high levels of performance on the other skill. In one study, a number of children aged 5 were each given eleven different tests of learning and memory. After the tests had been scored, the experimenters computed the correlations between each child's scores on all eleven tests. These were found to be very modest, averaging +0.14. Since correlations of this magnitude are virtually useless for making predictions about an individual child's scores, knowing that a particular child performed well (or badly) at one of the tasks of learning and remembering does not help us to predict how that child would fare on the other tasks.

Even psychologists who are firmly committed to the use of intelligence tests admit that there is no straightforward relationship between learning and measured intelligence. For example, Jensen (1978) notes that the correlations between measures of performance at a large number of simple learning tasks are meagre, and that the correlations between performance at learning tasks and scores on intelligence tests are also very small.

Despite the evidence, many people cling to the view that each person has a fixed capacity to learn, and that this capacity is closely related to intelligence. The fact that intelligence test scores are related to a person's learned achievements encourages us to believe that intelligence and learning must be connected. However, in investigations involving very simple forms of learning that are 'uncontaminated' by most of the broader influences that lead to some people being more successful as learners than others, such as previous knowledge, attentiveness, differences in motivation, the use of deliberate strategies, for example, it has been found that systematic differences in learning rate are remarkable only for their absence (Estes, 1970). Even when normal and mentally retarded individuals are compared, consistent differences in learning rates at tasks of 'pure' learning are hard to find.

Nor has it proved possible to identify any measure of learning rate that is basic to all kinds of learning. It used to be widely thought (Thorndike, 1931) that learning capacity depends upon the number of nerve connections that are available for forming new associations between items to be learned. A related view was that learning rate depended upon the speed with which information could be transmitted along networks of nerves: good learners were supposed to transmit information faster than slow learners. However, no firm evidence has been obtained to support theories of this kind. Undoubtedly, some people are more successful than others at particular learning tasks: in that sense it is realistic to speak of good and poor learners. But it would be wrong to assume that the differences between such people are caused by fundamental differences in the rates at which they are capable of learning.

It is not uncommon for test scores to be provided in the form of a profile which indicates the level of performance on each of a number of components of the test. Consequently, it is normally possible to discern whether a person performs better at, say, verbal tasks or spatial tasks. Nevertheless, intelligence test scores are not very informative about the reasons underlying a high or low level of performance. They do little to identify the causes of an individual's weaknesses, or to indicate the particular skills or abilities that a person would need to acquire in order to gain higher scores in the future.

One reason for this apparently paradoxical state of affairs is that, even in the absence of any fundamental variability in learning rate, in practical circumstances people are bound to differ considerably because the extensiveness of an individual's acquired skills and abilities will be affected by numerous factors that influence learning in one way or another. These include, in addition to motivational influences and differences in attentiveness and in the use of effective learning strategies, additional determinants of learning such as individual differences in perception, in perseverance, in impulsivity, a number of temperamental variables and a person's existing knowledge and skills. Since the latter have a cumulative, 'snowballing' influence upon the individual's learned achievements, it naturally follows that previous learning will affect a person's degree of success at new learning tasks, even in the absence of any differences in the (narrowly defined) rate of learning.

Influences that Contribute to High Capabilities

Why do some people, as learners, achieve far more than others? Of course, being highly intelligent is one important influence. But, as we have seen, differences in intelligence are not enough to account for differences between people in their capabilities. What other influences are especially crucial?

The determinants of high degrees of competence are numerous, and some of them are discussed in other chapters. For example, chapter 7 considers some of the many ways in which motivational influences help to determine a person's achievements. Other important contributing factors include the capacity to sustain one's attention on a task and resist distractions, and the ability to delay gratification (see chapter 1).

Practice and training are particularly important but sometimes underrated components of improvements in expertise. Few people deny that practice is necessary, but it is often not appreciated just how crucial it is. In fact, the highest levels of accomplishment at difficult areas of skill and expertise are never achieved in the absence of large amounts of practice and training. The sheer amount of practice needed in order for a person to become competent in any of a range of fields is very substantial. For example, to reach professional standards as a musical performer, or a bridge player, or a sportsperson or mathematician or scientist, periods of practice and training of the order of 10,000 hours or so are usually necessary. Ten thousand hours is a very considerable amount of time. It means the equivalent of around three hours per day for a ten-year period. That is a huge investment of time, of course, and it is hardly surprising that most people are unwilling or unable to devote such a huge chunk of their lives to one particular area of expertise.

Of course, the sheer time spent training or practising is not the only consideration. The appropriateness of the studying activities is another, and so is the learner's commitment. An hour spent going through the motions of practising a musical instrument is far from being equivalent to an hour in which the learner is dedicated to achieving improvements.

It is widely believed that there are a few fortunate individuals who can make progress effortlessly, without having to engage in the extensive practice and training that is essential in order for ordinary people to achieve high levels of expertise. However, this is simply untrue. The factual evidence indicates that high degrees of competence are virtually never gained without major investments of time and effort. Even in the case of geniuses such as Mozart and Einstein, close examination of their actual circumstances usually reveals very substantial amounts of time being committed to training activities and related experiences.

So training and practice are essential ingredients of high levels of competence. But why is it that some young people are able to sustain the necessary effort and concentration while others find that impossible? Why cannot everyone become an excellent mathematician or scientist, or even an expert tennis-player? Some research by one psychologist, Mihaly Csikszentmihalyi (pronounced 'Chicksent-mi-harlyee') and his co-researchers has helped to provide answers for those important questions (Csikszentmihalyi and Csikszentmihalyi, 1993). They worked with adolescent students and noticed that, among substantial numbers of apparently promising young people, some of them made good progress but others did not. Also, the individuals who did best were almost always young people who worked hard at their studies and devoted time to training and practising activities. But these researchers also observed that most adolescents do not seem to enjoy the practising and studying activities that are necessary for getting ahead. These are often solitary activities, and they demand and require sustained effort, as well as a strong measure of the capacity to delay gratification that was first mentioned in chapter 1. But young people are often not at all keen on spending their time in that way. They would rather do other things like watching television or hanging about with their friends.

And yet studying is the key to success, and *some* young people manage to do it. So it would be very useful to know what is different about the youngsters who are able to devote time to training and practising activities, in comparison with adolescents who seem unable to study.

Csikszentmihalyi decided that it would be helpful to assess how young people actually experienced various kinds of activities, including studying. When he did this he confirmed that, when quizzed about their feelings at particular times, the majority of young people when engaged in a studying activity reported that they were not enjoying what they were doing and that they did not feel particularly alert. When engaged in other activities, such as watching television with friends, the majority of the participants reported that they were enjoying what they were doing and felt considerably more alert.

However, there were some participants who were more positive when questioned while studying, and these were the ones who were making most progress. So Csikszentmihalyi and his colleagues were keen to discover how those individuals differed from the others. Why was it that they, unlike the others, were relatively happy to persevere with the study and practising activities that were so necessary for success?

Csikszentmihalyi was able to answer those questions because they had previously divided the adolescent participants into four groups on the basis of data obtained by the researchers concerning their home and family backgrounds. These were assessed on two separate dimensions. The first referred to the extent to which a young person's home background was mentally *stimulating*, as a consequence of the parents being good at providing opportunities for their children to learn and having high educational expectations. Understandably, it is helpful for a young person to have a stimulating home background.

Yet, having a family background that is mentally stimulating may not be enough. The family backgrounds of young participants were also rated on another dimension. This assessed the degree of the extent to which families were rated as providing their children with structure and support. A family rated high on this dimension would be one in which parents and siblings helped each other, and could depend upon one another, and in which there were clear rules and responsibilities. In such families youngsters knew what was expected of them and usually got on with it, confident that they could rely on getting support from others when that was needed. And they were good at delaying gratification, if only because they had got into the habit of doing so. In contrast, young people whose families did not reliably provide structure and support often wasted time complaining or squabbling, and arguing about whose turn it was to do a task or receive a favour, so they were less inclined to get on with whatever needed to be done.

Csikszentmihalyi and his colleagues asked what relationship, if any, existed between the children's membership of these categories and their feelings about study activities. With *non*-study activities, it was found that the adolescents' reactions were unrelated to family backgrounds. However, when the participants were asked about their feelings at times when they were supposed to be studying or practising, the responses did vary considerably. Those of most of the young people were highly negative. They definitely did not enjoy studying, or feel wide awake when they were supposed to be practising.

But some participants responded differently, reporting more favourably and describing themselves as more alert than the other participants. These young people strongly tended to belong to the category whose family backgrounds were described as being both stimulating and supportive. These adolescents, in contrast with those from the other three kinds of backgrounds (stimulating but not supportive, supportive but not stimulating, neither stimulating nor supportive) were relatively positive about studying. They reported enjoying it more. When they were studying alone they reported feeling alert and wide awake.

In short, there appear to be two features of a child's family background that incline a young person to be capable of persisting at the kinds of studying and practising activities that are essential in order to make good progress. Young people whose home backgrounds were both stimulating and supportive have a big advantage over others. They are more likely to do well, partly because they have acquired good working habits and learned to get on with the study-ing. This does not mean that young people from other kinds of background can never catch up, of course, but, at least for the time being, the youngsters in Csikszentmihalyi's study whose backgrounds were supportive and stimulating did have a real advantage.

The Assumed Roles of Innate Gifts and Talents

One common belief is that individuals who become unusually ca-pable within various specific skills of competence, ranging from art to mathematics and sports to literature, is that they are born possess-ing innate gifts or talents. The presence in a young person of such gifts is believed to make exceptional capabilities possible (Winner, 1996). In the absence of innate gifts and talents, extraordinary com-petence within various fields of attainment are simply not possible.

The belief that such innate gifts and talents exist and are neces-sary in order for a young person to excel has important practical implications. That is because the view of a teacher or other influen-tial adult that a child does or does not possess an innate gift is often introduced as a reason for deciding whether or not that child is to receive the kind of training opportunities that are needed in order to have a good chance of being especially successful. A child who is believed to possess an innate gift will be selected: a child who is not believed to have such a talent will be excluded.

Do innate gifts and talents actually exist? The question is an im-portant one, if only because if they do not, the practice of exclud-ing children from training opportunities on the basis of experts' belief that they lack such talents is clearly unfair and discriminatory.

As it happens, there is very little convincing evidence to support the widespread view that innate gifts and talents do exist (Sloboda, Davidson and Howe, 1994; Howe, Davidson and Sloboda, 1998). Many people who assume that they do justify that belief by assert-ing that individuals differ enormously in the extent to which they acquire expertise, and in the apparent ease in which they do so. Some writers have also drawn attention to the observation that children often already seem very different from one another while they are still young, and before they have had the formal training that might be expected to produce large differences in individuals. In other words, the usual justification for believing that innate gifts and talents do exist is that there are differences between young people which appear hard to explain.

This is hardly a satisfactory position. To assume that innate gifts and talents must be present just because of the existence of differences between individuals for which there is no obvious alternative explanation is nothing but lazy thinking. Only if it was possible to be really sure that no alternative explanation can be found would the case for innate gifts be a convincing one. And as it happens, as soon as one begins to make a serious search for alternative causes of the differences between people in their abilities, it becomes clear that such alternative causes are not at all hard to find.

In fact there are numerous possible reasons for the observation that young people differ in the ease with which they make progress within various fields of expertise (Howe et al., 1995, 1998; Sosniak, 1985, 1990). Most of these differences stem from children's varying experiences and diverging preferences, or from the different kinds of events they have been exposed to or the differing opportunities they have been given.

Even two children brought up in very similar environments may have remarkably different experiences. For example, in one family, a younger child will often perceive various happenings and events quite differently from an older child (Dunn and Plomin, 1990). Moreover, two children brought up in the same family may form distinct preferences at an early age. Thus, for instance, one child quickly acquires a liking for music, and regularly pays considerable attention to sounds, thereby gaining knowledge that will facilitate the acquisition of expertise at a musical instrument, while another child directs her attention to very different kinds of events, and fails to acquire the knowledge that could facilitate musical expertise. Perhaps the second child is more interested in physical activities, and consequently gains skills that might contribute to sporting competence. There is nothing at all mysterious about forming distinct preferences early in life: that is an almost inevitable consequence of the fact that different children's experiences are not identical (Renninger and Wozniak, 1985; see also Slater, 1995).

In short then, the trouble with assuming the existence of innate talents is that there are no convincing reasons for making that assumption and plenty of alternative explanations for those phenomena that are supposed to provide the evidence that talents do exist. An extensive survey of various finds of findings that can help answer the question of whether or not innate talents do exist led to the conclusion that there is no convincing evidence to confirm their existence and that there are various alternative explanations for the phenomena that have been cited in their support.

And yet decisions that have large effects upon the lives of numerous children are made on the assumption that the innate talent view is correct. Many children are excluded from valuable opportunities because of the (probably erroneous) beliefs of teachers or specialists who are responsible for making decisions about the allocation of scarce resources.

However, the fact that innate talents may be mythical rather than real does not exclude the possibility that inherited differences between people may have effects that influence their capabilities and their intelligence. It is possible, for example, that inherited differences in temperament have consequences that influence individuals' differing abilities. But it is reasonably clear that there do not exist inherited differences between individuals having the direct and inevitable influences that innate gifts and talents are often believed to have. The ways in which genetic influences have their effects on broad traits are rarely simple: typically, lengthy and complicated chains of interacting processes are involved.

Critical Periods

For many reasons, the first few years of life are extremely important for later development. A number of authors have expressed this view in a more extreme form, and have stated that the earliest years are so crucial that if certain skills are not acquired then, the child will be at a serious disadvantage throughout life.

So far as the acquisition of a child's first language is concerned, this may be true. But for most other kinds of learning the evidence indicates that it would be an exaggeration to state that certain early periods of a child's life are absolutely critical. Generally, if skills are not acquired at the normal time they can be learned later. It has been found that children who have become retarded as a result of appalling neglect and deprivation may regain most if not all of the lost ground if they receive intense stimulation and instruction in later years (Clarke and Clarke, 1976). Of course, there may be major advantages to learning something early in life. For example, some aspects of learning a second language may be much easier for a child who is too young to feel self-conscious about speaking in an unfamiliar tongue.

Everyone agrees that, as learners, children are very different from one another by the time they begin school. It is not always realized how deep-rooted are some of the individual factors that influence what a child learns. In fact, differences between children in a number of attributes that affect learning can be seen as early as the first year of life. Research with infants (Korner, 1971) has revealed that a variety of individual differences between infants, affecting either their activities or their perceptual abilities, can affect later experience and learning. For example, as soon as they are born, some infants cry more than others. Crying acts to bring about social contacts between mother and infant, and consequently differences between babies in their crying behaviour can influence caretaking by the mother and the accompanying social interactions. As a result, early social learning will be affected. Also, babies react differently to being soothed and picked up when they are crying. Some remain comforted for a long time; others soon require more attention. Differences in the way babies respond to caretaking may influence how mothers respond to their children. For instance, an inexperienced mother's feelings of competence may be strongly affected by the reactions to her attempts to soothe the baby. In turn, her feelings of success or failure may affect her actions in the future as she interacts with the child in the situations that determine the form of the child's earliest social learning.

Another early difference that can have a big influence on what a child learns is in what some researchers term cuddliness. Most babies are cuddly, but some infants do not seem to like being held and resist their mothers' attempts to hug or embrace them. These 'non-cuddlers' dislike physical constraints of any kind and they are more restless than other infants. Differences in the degree of cuddliness inevitably lead to differences in the way infants are handled, and influence the interactions that take place between mother and child (Schaffer and Emerson, 1964). The formation of social attachments may also be affected adversely. However, for those kinds of learning that involve limb movements, non-cuddlers have an advantage, resulting from their restlessness and high level of physical activity.

Individual differences in infants' perceptual sensitivity are a further cause of early differences in learning. Some infants seem to require more sensory stimulation that others. Babies who need a large amount of stimulation are described as having a high visual threshold. More sensitive infants, with lower visual thresholds, are overwhelmed and made anxious by too much sensory stimulation. The effects of differences in perceptual sensitivity may combine with those of early social differences, as in the following sequence of events. Young infants who cry often are frequently picked up. When infants are picked up they tend to become visually attentive, and gain experience of the visual world. Those infants who have high visual thresholds, who benefit from having extra visual stimulation, stand to gain more from the experience of being picked up than the more sensitive infants with low visual thresholds. For the latter, the effect of picking them up frequently may be to upset them by over-stimulation: they may receive all the visual stimulation they need without being picked up. In consequence, young infants will be affected in differing ways when their mothers pick them up. Conversely, some of the effects of maternal neglect, for instance, when a mother does not regularly pick up and play with her child, will be more severe for a child who has a high threshold than for a child who has more visual sensitivity. Children with a high visual threshold will be more adversely affected by not being picked up.

Such early differences can have long-lasting effects. For example, it has been found that infants who are physically active often become 5-year-olds with higher scores on tests of motor performance than on tests of verbal achievement (Escalona, 1973). It was also found that 5-year-old children who as infants were rated as being highly sensitive are good at communicating sensitively and precisely. These findings add weight to the view that in order to assess the effects of environmental factors upon a child, it is essential to know something about the way the individual experiences the events in his life.

Although the evidence does not support the view that there are definite critical periods for human learning, and shows that there is great flexibility in the ways in which development can take place, the sequencing of a child's experiences is crucial. A number of training studies have shown that timing and phasing of learning is highly important. For example, Burton White (1971), who studied the progress of infants towards gaining the ability to reach out for objects and pick them up, observed that what appears to be a simple feat depends upon the precise co-ordination of a number of sub-skills. White was interested in the possibility of accelerating babies' progress by providing an 'enriched' environment, but his first efforts were unsuccessful. He knew that visual attending was one important sub-skill, and he knew from previous work that showing infants bright visual objects would improve their attending skills. However, White found to his surprise that the effect of the visual stimuli he provided was to delay rather than accelerate the infants' acquisition of reaching skills. Subsequently, however, he discovered that he had mistakenly provided enrichment at an inappropriate time. His visual stimuli had encouraged the babies to look at the displays at a period in life when they would normally spend a good deal of time looking at their hands. For the young infant, looking at one's own hands is a very good way of starting to learn to integrate visual activities and hand movements, a form of co-ordination which is essential for picking up objects. In effect, White's enriching materials had retarded learning, not because they were ineffective but because they came at the wrong time and interfered with the acquisition of essential skills.

These and other findings show that a child's achievements at learning new skills will be strongly influenced by whether or not new skills have been introduced at appropriate times and in a logical order. Researchers have introduced terms such as optimum stimulation and the optimum match to indicate the importance of trying to mesh environmental stimulation with individual children's particular abilities and needs.

There was at one time a fairly widespread view that a child's eventual achievements were almost entirely determined by events in the first few years of life. Such a view rested on a misinterpretation of evidence that showed that the progress of children could be predicted reasonably well on the basis of their early childhood achievements. The fallacy lies in the assumption that because mature achievements can be predicted in advance to some extent, they must have been determined early in life. In fact, one reason why early achievements happen to be a good predictor of later achievements is that early achievements are a good indicator of the child's home circumstances. If a child is brought up during the early years in a loving home with parents who devote effort and expertise to helping the child to become an effective and independent learner, it is very likely that the child will achieve at a high level and it is also likely that the child will continue to receive the same environmental advantages in subsequent years.

7

— How Motivation Affects Learning —

Motivation and Success at School

The importance of motivation for school success cannot be exaggerated. However, the manner in which motivational factors influence learning is not always straightforward. It is not just a matter of a child wishing to achieve an eventual goal: if that were the case it might be hard to account for the numerous youngsters who would like to be brain surgeons or veterinarians but fail to do so. However strong the average 10-year-old's desire to become, say, a brain surgeon, in the absence of appropriate rewards and encouragement throughout the lengthy period between the initial wish to succeed and the eventual far-off attainment of success, the chances of such success are extremely slim.

The many aims, intentions, wants, drives, wishes, hopes and desires that comprise the motivational forces in a young person's life do not all work in the same direction. Moreover, many of the motives that guide students' classroom behaviour are largely outside the teacher's control. For example, the desire for approval of his or her peers has distracted many a child from working hard at school tasks.

The chances of success at those achievements that demand sustained effort throughout years of schooling are highest when young people can draw upon constant support and encouragement from their families. The value of long-term effort and planning for the future is most readily apparent to a child who can see at first-hand, perhaps in a brother or a sister, the rewards that come from persisting at arduous learning tasks.

Different needs are more or less important at different times. The hierarchical need system of Abraham Maslow illustrates the fact that some basic needs predominate over other motives, and that various wants and desires become more prominent as other needs are filled. According to Maslow, individuals act to satisfy basic physiological needs and the need for safety, and only when these are satisfied do other needs, for instance, for love and belonging and for self-esteem, become important. All children need plenty of encouragement and plenty of attention, and their need to know and understand predominates, according to Maslow's theory, only when all the other needs have been met.

So paying full attention to school learning tasks is probably easier for those children whose other needs are fully satisfied: they are free to direct their energies to meeting the need to 'know and understand'. However, it is equally true that success at school tasks may help a child to satisfy other needs, for instance, the need for self-esteem, or even love and belonging.

On the whole, children thrive on praise and encouragement. However, there are occasions on which too much praise, especially if it is not altogether appropriate, can have a negative influence. Children who are frequently praised for being clever or intelligent may come to believe that their successes stem from their inherent qualities, and fail to appreciate that solving problems usually depends upon persistent efforts. But a child who is explicitly praised for having succeeded as a result of trying hard will be more likely to get a message from that encouragement, and be motivated to keep on making efforts in the future.

Even rewards, if inappropriate, can have negative rather than positive consequences. In one study it was found that, when children who were already playing actively and with enjoyment were told that if they went on in the same manner they would be given 'Good Player' certificates, they became less active and creative than children not so rewarded. In another investigation, when a child's paintings were frequently praised by teachers, the paintings started to become less creative or original, and more conventional (Amabile, 1983).

A distinction can be made between external (or 'extrinsic') and internal (or 'intrinsic') kinds of motivation. In the above examples it is likely that inappropriate external rewards were interfering with activities that were being satisfactorily nurtured by intrinsic motivation that centred on the children's own interests. Broadly speaking, those students whose motivation to learn comes partly from their own curiosity and interests and their sheer enthusiasm for making progress are consequently more independent as learners than other students, and better equipped to get ahead on their own, without needing constant encouragement. Mature and independent students tend to have high levels of intrinsic motivation.

However, it does not follow that extrinsic motivation is unnecessary for mature learners. After all, everybody needs encouragement. Even people who are particularly creative and successful often want, and benefit from, praise and material rewards.

There needs to be a balance between internal and external motivating influences. When a learner is young and immature, and beginning to learn things that are still new or unfamiliar, it would be unrealistic for teachers to expect that the child's intrinsic motivation will be sufficiently strong to bear the main burden of providing incentives to learn. At this stage, at which learners need help with getting started on a new activity, plenty of praise and encouragement will be appreciated. At a later stage, when a degree of competence has already been achieved, it is likely that the learning activity will start to be more interesting and rewarding for its own sake, and at this stage too much emphasis upon external incentives would not be beneficial. But even then, most learners will still appreciate the external rewards that arise from making progress. Very few people can dispense with them entirely.

Achievement Motivation

The extent to which a person desires to do well influences their activities, and consequently their degree of success, in a wide range of circumstances. Of course, most young people want to succeed, and most make efforts to do so. However, there are substantial differences between individuals in the strength of their achievement motivation. These differences tend to be fairly stable, and children who try hard to succeed often become adults who are equally motivated to do well.

That does not mean that children inherit a given level of achievement motivation. Differences between individuals on this dimension seem to be largely acquired, as a consequence of a young person's early experiences. Achievement motivation tends to be strong in young people whose parents have been warm and supportive, have given their children plenty of rewards and encouragement, who have encouraged their children to be independent, outgoing and self-reliant, and to make their own decisions. But just encouraging independence and self-reliance is not enough, especially when the parents are negligent or fail to give their child enough support, or are too inclined to criticize. It is the combination of encouragement for independence and self-reliance with plenty of help and support that is crucial

Although the desire to achieve is widespread, the forms it takes differ not only between people but within the same individual at different times. A number of needs, which vary in strength, combine to form a general achievement motivation in learners. David Ausubel (1968) suggested that in a school setting achievement motivation has at least three components.

The first is *cognitive* drive. This refers to the motivational effects of a learner finding a task interesting, or relating to the individual's need for competence. The cognitive drive is 'task-oriented' in that the motive for attending to the task and becoming involved in the activity is intrinsic to the task itself. Some writers have claimed that schooling tends to destroy children's curiosity and the interest in learning that they display when they first enter school (Bruner, 1972; Bates, 1979).

The second component of achievement motivation in the classroom is an *ego-enhancing* one. For Ausubel, ego-enhancing factors are ones that refer to learners' feelings about status, self-esteem, being adequate and having success. These factors can motivate learning, but indirectly, through events that are external to the actual learning task, such as high marks, praise and other rewards. These factors can undoubtedly have a positive influence on learning, albeit an indirect one. However, since they largely depend upon other people, they do not make a contribution to the individual student's independence and self-control as a learner.

Thirdly, there are *affiliative* components of achievement motivation. These are directed towards bringing a person the approval of others. This source of influence may add to or oppose the effect of the other factors that contribute to achievement motivation. For instance, acting in a way that is designed to win the admiration of a child's peers and be accepted as 'one of the gang' may be incompatible with study behaviour activated by the cognitive drive.

Each of the three components of achievement motivation, cognitive, ego-enhancing and affiliative, can vary in both strength and direction. Their relative strengths change as children get older. In young children, for instance, the affiliative drive is very strong, and the attention of adults is important for them. That is one reason for the success of those behaviour modification techniques for classroom management in which the teacher's attention is contingent on good behaviour. In older children, the need for the teacher's attention is less strong, and consequently such techniques are considerably less effective. For the older child, the attention and approval of other pupils is likely to be at least as important as the teacher's attention.

Being in Control

A child's achievements are influenced by the extent to which he feels in control of his own learning processes. A number of factors, beginning in infancy, affect the young person's feeling of being in control. In the infant, the fact that responses are seen to have predictable outcomes contributes towards the beginnings of a sense of having mastery over the environment, rather than being entirely helpless. One writer has noted in his own infant the synchrony between responses and outcomes that is essential if a child is to start to gain a sense of control:

He sucks, the world responds with warm milk. He pats the breast, his mother tenderly squeezes him back. He takes a break and coos, his mother coos back. He gives a happy chirp, his mother attempts to chirp back. Each step he takes is synchronized with a response from the world. (Seligman, 1975, p. 139)

Normally, the child learns that in a gradually increasing range of circumstances his own actions matter: they have outcomes that influence the environment. But, for a variety of reasons, individual differences arise in children's experiences of control over their own lives. Extreme instances of lack of such control are found in what Martin Seligman (1975) terms *learned helplessness*. Seligman has drawn attention to the results of experiments on human and animal subjects showing that when an organism does not have control over what happens to it, and learns that it has no control, it becomes unresponsive and passive, learns poorly and fails to display normal social behaviours.

Some of the symptoms that we associate with the state of depression in adults are regarded by Seligman as being related to learned helplessness. He notes some similarities between the behaviour of a depressed person – isolated, withdrawn, passive and indecisive – and the behaviour of animals in whom learned helplessness has been induced by placing them in circumstances in which their actions are not reliably followed by predictable outcomes, and thus exert no effective control over the environment.

The extent to which a child is able to control various aspects of life is important for later development, as is the extent to which he feels himself to be in control. A number of researchers have examined the implications for school learning of a child's beliefs about the control of events. The concept of *locus of control* refers to a person's general expectancy for events that affect the individual to be controlled by internal or external factors (Rotter, 1975). A person perceives control to be internal when he believes that events or outcomes depend on his own behaviour or personal characteristics, such as ability. A person is said to perceive events as being externally controlled if he believes them to be caused by factors that are beyond his control, such as luck, fate or the actions of other people.

A child's perceptions about locus of control are largely determined by past experiences. Children who perceive the control of their own activities as being largely internal rather than external are more likely than others to report that their parents were supportive and affectionate, and more generous with praise than with criticism (Collier, 1994). Equally important, perceptions about locus of control affect the child's approach to learning. The belief by a child that the outcome of a situation depends on his or her own actions makes it more likely that the child will introduce and persist at those kinds of behaviour that lead to successful learning. Such a child will be more likely to attend to the task, to rehearse, to introduce appropriate learning strategies and so on than a child who believes that outcomes and rewards are caused by external factors.

The perceived locus of control is not the only factor influencing a child's approach to a task. The child's perception of the value of the outcome is equally crucial. A child may believe (correctly) that the chances of getting high marks in a test depend upon the time spent studying, but unless the same child places a high value upon a good test score this perception may fail to influence studying (Stipek and Weisz, 1981).

Locus of control is correlated with school achievement: high achievement levels are associated with the perception of control as being internal. However, although this finding is consistent with the view that perceiving control to be internal positively influences achievement at school, it is not inevitable that any such cause-and-effect relationship exists. Conceivably, the correlation could be due to achievements having an influence on perceived locus of control, or to both factors being affected by some (unknown) third variable. It is possible, for instance, that when children are successful at school they perceive themselves as being the cause of their success (internal control) whereas when they are less successful they blame outside influences (external locus of control).

As it happens, the findings of carefully controlled studies that have been undertaken to examine this and other possibilities show that locus of control does influence achievement. This does not entirely rule out the additional possibility that achievement may have some effect upon perceived locus of control, but the main influence is in the opposite direction.

The effects of altered locus of control

If a child's perceptions of locus of control can be altered, it ought to be possible to raise school achievement. Does that actually happen? Some interesting classroom experiments have shown that changing children's perceptions of control can have exciting positive effects. In one study (Matheny and Edwards, 1974) twenty-five classroom teachers followed careful instructions to give the young children greater responsibility for organizing their own learning activities. This led to a very large improvement in performance at reading, and it was also noted that the largest effects occurred in classrooms where the teachers were judged to have been most successful in following the instructions.

In another classroom experiment 6-year-old children who had previously been told by the teacher exactly when to do various kinds of school work were allowed to decide for themselves on the timing of the various tasks, although the choice of the tasks remained with the teacher (Wang and Stiles, 1976). The change resulted in a higher proportion of assignments being completed. Allowing children to choose for themselves the order in which tasks were done also gave them an increased feeling of control (as indicated by interview reports) over their learning at school.

Findings such as these demonstrate that giving children greater control over their educational experiences can lead to very real improvements in school learning. There are some uncertainties concerning the detailed interpretation of the results. For example, it is not entirely clear whether the beneficial effects are due to differences in locus of control as such, or to differences in perception of control locus, or to both or to other factors that the experiments failed to control. Whatever the answers, however, it is very likely that the factors manipulated in studies of classroom control are ones that are of great practical importance.

Another incompletely resolved issue concerns the possibility that different types of internal and external control have different effects. For example, Stipek and Weisz (1981) note that an analysis based on attribution theory would point to the fact that a child who thinks that his failure is due to lack of ability (perceived internal locus of control) will act differently after failure at a learning task than a child who thinks that the failure is due to not trying (again, perceived internal locus of control).

Locus of control and student mastery

It is highly probable that the effectiveness of a variety of successful educational experiments, innovations and reforms has been due at least in part to children gaining greater control over the circumstances in which they learn. Instances include the beneficial effects associated with mastery learning and (observed in some investigations, but not all) with open-plan classrooms. An especially important element of changes in the locus of control is the fact that individuals are allowed to make choices for themselves.

Altered perceptions of control may have been a key factor in the success of a project in which high-school student volunteers, who were themselves poor readers, were paid to tutor younger backward readers (Cloward, 1967). The most striking finding was not that the younger children's reading scores improved (they actually gained six months' growth over a five-month period in which they were tutored four hours per week, compared with 3.5 months' growth, on average, by students in a control group), but that the tutors' own reading standard improved considerably. The tutors gained an average of 3.4 years in reading skills, over the seven-month period during which they participated in the experiment, compared with a gain of 1.7 years by students in a control condition. Gains in self-esteem and greater student control over reading activities probably contributed to this very real improvement.

Pawns and origins

Another classroom investigation of the effects of changing children's perceptions of locus of control was undertaken by R. de Charms (1976). He distinguishes between perceiving oneself as a 'pawn' who is controlled largely by external forces or as an 'origin'. An origin is a person who regards his actions as being caused by his own free choices and wishes, and consequently assumes responsibility for his activities and achievements.

De Charms considers that schooling influences children's perceptions of themselves as being pawns or origins. To test some of his ideas he conducted an experiment in which black inner-city children (aged 12 to 14 years) in the United States were encouraged to assume more control of their own activities in the classroom and to take responsibility for their own actions. Their teachers were trained to teach the children to perceive themselves as being origins, and largely in charge of their own lives and responsible for their successes and failures, rather than being pawns, mere instruments of outside influences. The teaching was not only effective in altering the children's thinking about themselves in the direction of greater emphasis on their being origins rather than pawns, but it also had a positive influence on school achievement.

Self-efficacy

A final dimension of motivation, and one that is related to achievement motivation, locus of control and fear of failure, is what Albert Bandura (1986) calls *self-efficacy*. This refers to a person's belief in having the power to succeed. It is entirely possible for two individuals to possess similar capabilities and yet be very different in the extent to which they feel themselves to be capable of doing well.

Belief in one's own capabilities is obviously a useful attribute, and it is linked to various positive outcomes, encouraging individuals to be adventurous and ambitious. Young people with low self-efficacy tend to avoid challenges and miss out on opportunities. It diminishes the likelihood of an individual making positive changes. For example, some young smokers convince themselves that is their inability to refuse cigarettes from their friends which prevents them giving up the habit (Durkin, 1995). As with other motivational traits, family background is an important influence; unsurprisingly, the children of mothers who were depressed perceived themselves as ineffective at helping other young people deal with their emotional problems (Garber, Braafledt and Zeaman, 1991).

Success and Failure in the Classroom

Closely related to a person's perceptions about the factors that control important aspects of life are experiences of success and failure. It was mentioned previously that one beneficial effect of mastery learning is to induce an increased feeling of being personally in control over learning experiences. At least equally important are the effects on a person's self-perceptions of failing or being successful. Experiences of succeeding or failing inevitably contribute to a child's assessments of his own ability and to expectancies concerning success in the future. The very perceptions that we have regarded as forming barriers to a child's being successful at school, that is, of being externally controlled or of having the role of a pawn rather than an origin, can alternatively be seen as providing effective devices for maintaining one's self-esteem. If one is constantly failing, it is comforting to believe that forces outside one's control are responsible.

What happens to a child at school who encounters failure after failure? Some indications are given by the results of an experiment in which the subjects experienced repeated failure (Covington and Omelich, 1981). In fact, failure led to the participants having lower estimates of their ability, and in turn they became less happy, more shameful and less confident of future success. With the accumulation of further failures they became increasingly distressed, they experienced feelings of hopelessness and they became anxious to attribute their failure to external factors if it was at all possible to do so. When other strategies for maintaining self-esteem in the face of failure were no longer effective, signs of inaction and hopelessness became common.

The investigators note that a strategy of being inactive, which is not uncommonly observed in children at school by frustrated teachers and which might seem to be self-defeating, since it usually leads to failure, is actually very effective for some children. Such a strategy 'at least offsets the personal, shame-evoking implications of low ability' (Covington and Omelich, 1981, p. 806). For a student who has little confidence in success, is anxious not to fail in future attempts to learn and is perhaps not particularly interested in the topic being studied, being passive may well be the best way of dealing with the situation.

It is worth drawing attention to the fact that the participants in the above experiment were college students: the effects of failure on young children or individuals who are less knowledgeable and less confident about their learning abilities might well have been even more devastating. It is also pertinent that although the duration of the experiment was relatively long – several weeks – the time span was considerably less than that in which failures can mount in a child's day-to-day experience of life at school.

Some Conclusions

So far as school learning is concerned, there are two vital conclusions about motivation. First, it is extremely important. It makes an enormous difference to a young person's chances of success in almost all learning situations, and it is extremely rare to find individuals who achieve very high levels of accomplishment without being strongly motivated.

Secondly, motivation is not a straightforward single thing. There are many kinds and varieties of motivational influences, and their various effects depend upon a number of factors, including the kind of activity involved and its meaning and implications to the individual concerned. Different motivating influences can work together, with one another, or they can work against each other. Fears and anxieties can hold young people back even when they are very keen to succeed. A lack of confidence in one's capacity to do well, or a fear of failure, can impede a young learner just as effectively as an absence of knowledge or mental skills.

8

Reading, Comprehension and Learning

Throughout most of our lives, we frequently depend upon being able to learn from what we read, and the capability to do that with materials is among the most important of all the skills taught at school. But even understanding written information can be difficult. It demands the capacity to combine a number of the learning skills described in earlier chapters. Many young people leave school with limited expertise in learning from passages of text.

There are close ties between learning, reading and comprehension (Marton, 1981). We have looked at some of the devices that learners use to help them understand new materials. Making good use of one's existing knowledge is particularly crucial: people regularly depend upon whatever they already know in order to make sense of new information. The existing knowledge may be in the form of data about the attributes of a single item or event, or it may take the form of a large schema containing highly organized information about a regularly encountered sequence of events, such as going to a restaurant or travelling on a bus.

As we have already seen, students can do various things to aid understanding. For example:

1 Information that is unfamiliar can sometimes be made easier to comprehend by providing a heading or title, as was shown in chapter 5. A title may direct the reader to something that he or she already knows that will clarify the meaning of the new information.
2 Alternatively, as we have also seen, when new information can-

not readily be connected to existing knowledge, it may be possible to make advance organizers which help perform that function. The successful learner is good at finding links between existing knowledge and new materials: becoming able to do that is an important aspect of learning how to learn.

3 Activities such as rehearsal, self-testing and making summaries can all contribute to the success of a person's efforts to make use of existing knowledge in order to assist new learning.

4 Finally, making good use of existing knowledge depends upon the learner having the necessary retrieval skills and being able to apply or transfer old skills and knowledge to new circumstances.

Helping Students to Understand

Teachers can do much to improve children's ability to comprehend text, as has been demonstrated in some highly successful training projects. Many researchers have investigated comprehension skills, and it has proved possible to devise training methods that can produce substantial practical gains in students' success at understanding written information.

Even relatively simple activities on the part of students can improve some aspects of comprehension. Note-taking, for example, can be helpful (as we shall discover in chapter 9), especially when learners express information in their own words rather than copying what they read word for word (Howe, 1977). Students who undertake study activities such as underlining or taking notes gain more benefit from a period of study than students who are inactive (Brown and Smiley, 1978).

An individual's understanding of new information will naturally be influenced by the manner in which it is presented. The importance of the content is obvious enough: few 10-year-olds will make sense of a passage from a textbook in advanced physics, because they lack too much of the knowledge necessary for comprehension. But a child's understanding is also affected by the structure of prose materials. For example, young children find stories easier to understand if they conform to the familiar, 'well-formed' structure of a traditional tale.

Effective study activities and the use of existing knowledge go hand in hand. The likelihood of an activity making a useful contribution to learning depends upon the learner's ability to make effective use of what is already known (Brown and Smiley, 1978). These authors found that students only benefited from activities such as note-taking or underlining when they were capable of identifying the important points in the information.

A tried and tested way to improve a student's understanding of the information in a prose passage is to insert questions in the material. Teachers in the classroom often ask questions, and there are many good reasons for doing so. Numerous research studies have demonstrated the value of questions for improving learning and comprehension of information presented in prose form. Also, the effectiveness of the programmed learning systems of instruction that were favoured by educators in the 1960s depended heavily on the fact that students had to respond to frequent questions about the content being taught.

The word *mathemagenics* was introduced by E. Rothkopf (1970) as a general term for study activities that promote learning, such as reading, asking questions, inspecting items, attending to the teacher and mentally reviewing learned materials. Much of Rothkopf's research has concentrated on examining the effects of encouraging readers to answer questions that are embedded in passages of prose. Questions inserted into text can undoubtedly help students to master the specific information that is tested by the questions.

There is less certainty about the effects of inserted questions on the learning and comprehension of those aspects of a passage that are not specifically tested. Some studies have found definite improvements, others have not. Factors such as the positioning of the questions (in particular, whether a question appears before or after the part of the passage to which it refers) and their number and density are also important. The effects of these additional factors depend upon the content and form of the particular learning material in which they are inserted, and also upon individual matters such as the interest level and the degree of difficulty experienced by the particular learner.

Coding and Comprehending

Teachers have many ways of helping children to understand materials that are new and unfamiliar. They ask questions, demonstrate their own curiosity, assist children to predict what will happen next in a story and try to activate children's background knowledge. Teachers can also help to maximize learning by tailoring messages to the children's own level, questioning their assumptions, encouraging them to make inferences, directing attention to the main points and requiring children to make their thoughts and ideas explicit (Brown, Palincsar and Armbruster, 1984). These authors draw attention to the fact that, for a number of reasons, the young children who need the greatest amount of help in comprehending the materials they read often receive less assistance than children whose early efforts have been more successful.

Why is that? One reason is related to the fact that the efforts of teachers to help children learn to understand take place in the context of learning to read, reading and comprehension being inseparable. The evidence shows that those children who make the slowest progress at learning to read, and are relatively unsuccessful, are often given instruction which gives emphasis to the decoding aspects of learning to read rather than to comprehension. Understandably, teachers who are faced with children who are not well prepared for learning to read, or who are not progressing well and seem to lack basic skills, may decide to give remedial instruction that emphasizes the basic decoding skills that these children lack. Brown and her co-authors note that disadvantaged pupils are often taught to read by instructional programmes that emphasize decoding skills, whereas advantaged children are typically exposed to reading programmes that put more stress on comprehension.

In consequence, differences in children's preparedness for reading when they begin school may lead to differences in the kind of instruction they receive. In particular, disadvantaged and less successful students tend to be taught in ways that give less emphasis to comprehension. Good readers are often made to think about the meaning of the information they are reading. They are frequently asked to criticize passages and evaluate stories. Poor readers, on the other hand, get less practice at reading aloud, partly to avoid the embarrassment of repeated failure. Their reading exercises give more emphasis to pronunciation and decoding.

This has unfortunate consequences, even though it is quite understandable that a teacher should decide to give increased emphasis to decoding and other basic skills when a child is making little progress at learning to read. There are good practical reasons for doing that. Unfortunately, however, the resulting reduction in the time and effort that is spent helping these children to acquire comprehension skills tends to increase their problems with understanding what they read. So these students may learn some necessary reading skills but at the same time they make little progress towards becoming able to actually learn from reading.

The Skills of Comprehension

What does a child have to do in order to comprehend written information? And how can this be taught? Some of the more important component skills have been described by Allan Collins and Edward Smith (1982). These authors start by stating that if cognitive psychologists can specify in sufficient detail the processes that underlie thinking skills it will then be possible to devise effective methods for teaching students to master the skills. Collins and Smith next attempt to list what people need to learn, if they are to comprehend passages of prose. Basically, two kinds of comprehension skills have to be acquired.

The first group of skills are comprehension-monitoring abilities. The reader invokes these skills in order to keep a check on his ongoing comprehension processes as he reads, to be aware when they break down and to take some effective action to remedy the situation whenever they do so. In other words, readers ask themselves, 'Do I understand?' and if the answer is negative, they take appropriate action.

The second category of comprehension capabilities consists of ones that are necessary for making and evaluating estimates concerning the actual meaning of the material being read ('What's happening here?'). The capacity to do that is related to a student's ability to use various items of information in the text as clues for deciding on what is happening or predicting what is coming next (for example, 'X is going to rob the bank'). As new evidence arrives from the material that is being read, the reader evaluates earlier guesses and predictions. If they turn out to be wrong they can be adjusted or revised.

Monitoring

Comprehension monitoring enables the reader to become aware quickly of failure to understand the material. There can be various kinds of such failures. These include failure to understand particular words, failure to understand particular sentences, failure to understand relations between sentences and failure to understand how the text fits together as a whole.

Failures to understand words form the simplest kind of comprehension problem. They can occur either when a word is new or unfamiliar to the reader, or when the word does not make sense to the reader in the context in which it appears.

There are a number of possible reasons for a reader failing to understand a single sentence. For instance, a person may not be able to think of any interpretation of the sentence that makes sense. Alternatively, the sentence may seem to be ambiguous, and have more than one possible meaning. Another possible reason for a reader failing to understand a sentence is that the content may seem to be too vague to have any clear meaning. A final cause of difficulties is that the meaning of the sentence may seem to conflict with the reader's prior knowledge.

Similarly, there are a number of possible reasons for a person being unable to understand how one sentence relates to another or failing to see how the whole text fits together. A child's guess at the meaning of one sentence may clash with the interpretation of an earlier one. Research by Ellen Markman (1979) and others has shown that children (and older students as well) often fail to detect inconsistencies in text passages. Comprehension failures can also be caused by a child's being unable to see the point of some of the material, or to understand why characters act in the way that is described.

There are a number of remedial actions that readers can take when a comprehension failure occurs. Some of these actions are easy to apply, without disrupting reading, but others can be undertaken only at the cost of losing the thread of the passage. The least disruptive action is simply to ignore the failure to comprehend, and read on. This may be a sensible thing to do when the failure concerns a word or passage that is not critical for understanding the text as a whole, but in other circumstances ignoring a comprehension failure may have damaging consequences.

Secondly, it may be wise to adopt a 'wait and see' strategy. That involves suspending judgement about how to react to the comprehension failure, in the expectation that the meaning will soon become clearer. Again, in some instances this way of handling the problem will be effective: it certainly avoids disrupting the flow of reading. On other occasions, however, this rather passive approach will only lead to difficulties being confounded.

Third, the reader may try to work out what the material means, by making a guess that can be verified or disconfirmed at a later stage. Fourth, the reader can decide that an even more vigorous response to the failure to understand is necessary, and reread the passage that caused difficulties. Such an action has a definite cost for the reader, however, because it disrupts the reading process. Consequently it introduces the risk of losing the thread of the content.

Fifth, if it seems necessary to do so, the reader can take the bigger and inevitably more disruptive step of going back to a previous part of the text. If there is an overload of information, or if there seems to be a contradiction with some material that appeared earlier in the passage, a highly active response such as this may be essential if the meaning of the prose material is to be clarified.

The sixth and final remedial action suggested by Collins and Smith, and the most disruptive of all, is to seek outside help in order to make clear what something means. The source of help might be a dictionary or another book, or a person such as a teacher. This kind of action will undoubtedly interrupt the flow of the passage, but it may be the only way to discover the meaning of a word, a sentence or a larger segment that is crucial for understanding the text as a whole.

Some educators have suggested that too much comprehension monitoring can hinder reading by interfering with it. Collins and Smith disagree. They argue that, on the contrary, continuous monitoring may be necessary on some occasions, if the reader is to gain the full meaning from difficult materials that need to be mastered in detail. They also note, incidentally, that experienced readers may monitor some prose passages automatically, without making any conscious effort to do so. So while it is true that too much monitoring may occasionally cause problems for some readers, too little monitoring is more commonly a cause of failures to understand.

Generating and evaluating hypotheses

The activity of making hypotheses about the meaning of a passage, and evaluating them, forms the second of the two components of comprehension which Collins and Smith draw to the attention of teachers. Readers need to make guesses and form tentative hypotheses about the meanings of particular words and sentences. Also, it is equally important for a reader to make more general hypotheses about wider aspects of the text, for instance, about the intentions of story characters.

The capable reader makes various kinds of predictions as the text progresses. In order to understand written materials, students need to learn to make hypotheses or informed guesses about future content. Especially with fiction, readers need to be able to make use of any information in the text that helps to make it possible for such predictions to be made.

To help readers, the author may give details about a character that are designed to create expectations in the reader about the character's actions. For example, describing a particular character as having a 'curling lip' provides a clue to his role in a story. The author assumes that the reader will be able to interpret clues concerning (in this case) 'bad guys' and other elements in the text, and will form expectations about their future activities.

Expectations about the general contents of a story are also influenced by information about the situations that the story's characters encounter. A description of a funeral will set up the expectation that people will be sad: the information that a character has gained some kind of success or conquest, or won a prize, creates an expectation of happiness. Giving details about a character's goals or interests is another way of creating expectations. Similarly, providing the information that two characters in a story are in conflict or competition also leads to expectancies on the part of the reader. Particular kinds of genres, such as Westerns, detective stories and romantic fiction, for instance, all have special conventions that produce particular expectations.

Children learn to make predictions as they read a narrative passage. A story would appear very disjointed to a reader who found it impossible to make any such guesses or predictions. As we have seen, readers rely heavily on their existing knowledge in order to understand a narrative, and children as well as adults make sense of things by allocating meanings that are plausible in the particular context in which items of information occur. Recall that the reader who encounters the phrase 'held up his hand' will decide what it means by making an inference on the basis of that part of that reader's existing knowledge to which he or she is being directed by the context. The surrounding parts of the passage being read will normally provide clues about the author's intended meaning.

If the reader's knowledge includes a highly organized script or schema relating a particular kind of event (going to a theatre or a restaurant, for example) and if the reader has learned that a particular piece of information in the text provides a cue for eliciting such a script, then a story passage may be entirely meaningful even if it excludes much of the information about the detailed activities contained in the script. The author's intention is that the reader will supply for himself the necessary script information. Consequently, a novel might contain, say, a three-page narrative about two people who are sharing a meal in a restaurant, but which mentions hardly any of the meal-related events that actually took place. Nevertheless, the narrative will be entirely understandable. But for this to be possible it is essential that the reader has learned the appropriate comprehension skills. The reader must correctly interpret, consciously or otherwise, the cues in the text that direct him to the appropriate part of his prior knowledge and 'fill in' various items of information concerning eating meals in restaurant that are not mentioned in the narrative.

Teaching Comprehension Strategies

How are comprehension strategies best taught? What are the most effective ways to teach students to avoid comprehension failures in reading, and to remedy them when they do occur? How can learners utilize cues in the text in order to form good hypotheses and make accurate predictions? Collins and Smith recommend that the teaching should be done in three stages.

In the first stage, they suggest, the teacher should demonstrate or model the process of comprehending, by providing a kind of running commentary on the comprehension activities that he or she undertakes while reading aloud to a student. The second stage involves students being encouraged to do these things for themselves, and being given guidance whenever necessary as they read aloud. In the third stage the students practise using their newly gained comprehension skills while they read silently.

Stage One

The activities that the teacher should demonstrate in the modelling stage are ones that we have already described. As the teacher reads aloud, she can generate (aloud) any reasonable hypotheses (for instance, 'He's a bad guy'). Collins and Smith suggest that, up to a point, the more wrong hypotheses that are generated the better. Young students need to learn that hypotheses contribute to comprehension even if they do not turn out to be correct: revising and altering wrong hypotheses is a necessary aspect of comprehension.

The teacher should also try to make it clear why she is offering a particular hypothesis. And at a later point in the text, when new evidence that confirms or negates the hypothesis is encountered, the teacher should draw attention to this evidence, indicating its bearing upon the hypothesis. If the new evidence causes the teacher to alter a hypothesis, she should point out why and how it is being changed.

Another comprehension activity to which the teacher can draw students' attention in the modelling stage is noticing items in the text that appear to be incongruous or hard to understand. For example, when he or she does not understand a word or a sentence, or is unsure how two pieces of information are related, it is useful to draw attention to the problem, describing the source of the difficulty and stating how it arises. The teacher can then say aloud how she is attempting to deal with the situation (usually by trying one of the remedial procedures described above). The teacher can also voice aloud any other points that affect understanding of the passage; for instance, insights about the author's intentions, views about the effectiveness of the text, criticisms of the structure or contents, or suggestions about ways in which the text could be made clearer.

In brief, at this stage the teacher is performing aloud the various kinds of (normally silent) mental activities that contribute to comprehension. The purpose is to help students to realize just what kinds of activities are involved in the comprehension aspect of reading, to see how they are actually performed with a real piece of textual material and how the various different activities each contribute to making the text understandable.

Stage Two

In the second stage students are encouraged to generate their own hypotheses and perform other comprehension activities for themselves. Collins and Smith suggest that the teacher should start by suggesting possible hypotheses, for instance, 'Do you think X will do Y?' Next, the teacher should introduce questions that prompt students to form their own hypotheses, for instance, 'What do you think will happen to X?' or 'How do you think the story will end?' Gradually, students begin to generate their own hypotheses spontaneously, without the teacher's constant support.

The teacher can also encourage the students to take an increasingly active role in monitoring comprehension. Instead of the teacher drawing attention to a difficulty, as in the modelling stage, the students themselves begin to do so. They are encouraged to spot comprehension failures and problems and suggest possible remedies. The authors suggest that students who are given enough encouragement will come to contribute freely to each of the various comprehension activities. In this way, reading becomes a game in which the students all make guesses and predictions and then discover who was right.

Stage Three

In the third stage, the goal is to have students undertaking comprehension activities independently and silently. Here the teacher introduces various techniques to discover how the students are getting on. For example, in order to assess children's ability to detect sources of difficulty, the teacher may announce that there is something 'wrong' with the text, and ask the pupils to try and spot what it is. To assess their choice of remedies, the teacher might give the students prose materials in which problems have been deliberately inserted. She can then discover how the students cope with the difficulties they encounter.

Also, inserted questions can be introduced in order to assess a student's skill at making predictions about future text contents while reading silently. With a specially constructed text it is also possible to measure students' competence at forming and testing various different kinds of expectations and hypotheses about future contents.

Evaluating Comprehension Training

The effectiveness of teaching techniques very similar to the methods suggested by Collins and Smith has been evaluated in an interesting study by Ann Brown, Annemarie Palincsar and Bonnie Armbruster. They taught comprehension skills to American children aged 12 to 13 years who were, at the outset, very poor at comprehending written materials.

The planning of this research was strongly influenced by the authors' views about the acquisition of comprehension abilities. One important factor was their belief that situations in which the child has some kind of dialogue with an adult, typically the mother, are particularly effective for helping the child to acquire language and to make sense of important aspects of the world. Similar dialogues, involving sequences of close interaction in which the adult helps the child to learn by providing activities that serve to give feedback and to select and focus experiences, are seen by Brown and her colleagues as being central to a child's gaining the capacity to comprehend information that is presented in any of a number of forms, including written text. These authors also believe that, in order to help children to learn to understand prose materials, the teacher should undertake activities that include making statements aimed at activating relevant existing knowledge and questioning students' basic assumptions, in addition to using the specific teaching devices that are proposed by Collins and Smith. Brown and her colleagues list a number of activities that help readers understand written materials. These are:

1 Making the purposes of reading clear, and understanding the explicit and implicit demands of the task.
2 Activating relevant information from the reader's existing knowledge.
3 Directing attention effectively in order to focus concentration on the major content rather than less important details.
4 Evaluating content for internal consistency and compatibility with prior knowledge and common sense.
5 Monitoring ongoing activities in order to check that the text is being understood, by engaging in activities such as self-testing and periodically reviewing the content.
6 Drawing and testing kinds of inferences, including interpretations, predictions and conclusions.

The training studies

Brown and her colleagues decided to concentrate on training four specific skills: summarizing, questioning, clarifying and predicting. Each of these skills can be regarded as an important element of learning how to learn.

A crucial aspect of these instructional programmes is that all the different component activities are taught and utilized together. The authors point out that, while we know a great deal about the use of these activities in isolation, we know very little about the ways in which they can be combined in order to deal with comprehension failures.

In the training studies each of the above skills was utilized in order to respond to concrete problems encountered in comprehending actual text materials. Summarizing was carried out in order to report what had already been described in the text and to test for understanding. Clarifying occurred when a reader was confused about the meaning of a passage. Questioning was used as a concrete task, and it was always tied to a part of the text.

The training procedure was also designed to incorporate certain aspects of a dialogue between mother and child. There was considerable interaction between student and teacher, and much reciprocal questioning, paraphrasing, clarifying and predicting. There were three training studies in all. In the first two of them an investigator worked with the children, individually or in pairs. The third study was conducted by regular teachers in the school classroom.

Study One

The first study began with a number of assessment procedures, designed to measure as accurately as possible the students' initial comprehension skills and their weaknesses before the training started. The actual training period lasted for about three weeks. Six months later the students were tested again, and afterwards they received some further training. Four students participated as subjects in the study.

During the training period, a typical procedure involved the investigator and a student engaging together at an interactive learning game in which each of them took turns to lead a dialogue concerning the text passage they were reading. Thus both the investigator and the student took turns to 'teach' the successive paragraphs. With a new passage, the investigator might start by drawing attention to the title, and asking the student to make predictions about the contents and think about the possible relationship of the passage to the student's existing knowledge. Next, the student and the investigator silently read the first paragraph. Then the partner whose turn it was to 'teach' that segment would summarize it aloud, discuss and clarify any difficulties, invent a test question about the passage of the kind that a teacher might ask and, finally, make a prediction about the content of the remainder of the text.

The investigator would try to ensure that all these events were embedded in a reasonably natural dialogue, with each partner giving feedback to the other. The students were carefully told why each of the activities was useful. They were shown how all the different mental activities contributed to the ability to understand written materials.

The students did not find it at all easy at first to take their part in the dialogue. The adult had to give them a good deal of help, based on prompting techniques, praise and encouragement, and detailed feedback. In the earliest sessions the students were relatively passive, and the investigator spent much of the time modelling effective strategies. As the sessions progressed, however, the students became increasingly expert at leading the dialogue. Here are some examples of the remarks and comments that were contributed by the investigator:

> If you're having a hard time summarizing, why don't you think of a question first?
> You asked that question well; it was very clear what information you wanted.
> A question I would have asked would be. . .

The training was extremely successful. Findings obtained from a number of objective measures showed that the procedures were highly effective. For example, in the first sessions 46 per cent of the questions produced by the students were either judged not to be proper questions or needed clarification, but by the final sessions only 2 per cent of the responses were in this category. Similarly, the percentage of students' summaries that were judged to have captured the main ideas rose from 11 per cent to 60 per cent. By the later sessions the students' own questions were similar to those constructed by the teacher, and used the questioner's own words rather than just repeating words in the textual passage.

To provide an independent measure of the effectiveness of the comprehension skills the students were also questioned about prose passages which they read on their own, outside the training sessions. At the beginning, their success rate averaged only 15 per cent. This rose to over 80 per cent during the training sessions. When the students were tested six months later the number of correct answers averaged 60 per cent, and their rate of success rose again to over 80 per cent after just one day of renewed training.

The students were also given a social studies comprehension test in their own classroom, administered by the classroom teacher, in order to assess the generalization of their newly acquired comprehension skills to the classroom setting. At the beginning of the study, their scores had placed them in the bottom 15 per cent of seventh-grade students for comprehension skills. By the end of the training, however, each student rose to a higher percentile rank. The increases for the four students were respectively 20 per cent (i.e. moving from the fifteenth percentile of students of that age to the thirty-fifth percentile), 46 per cent, 4 per cent and 34 per cent.

In summary, the findings of a number of separate tests, in the students' regular classroom as well as in the training environment, all demonstrated substantial improvements in comprehension. The training was highly successful.

Studies Two and Three

The second study was similar to the first one in most respects, but it also included a number of tests that were designed to measure transfer of the trained skills to comprehension activities such as detecting errors in texts and rating the relative importance of different parts of a narrative. Again, the training was highly successful. Of the six students in the second study, none of whom averaged more than 40 per cent on comprehension tests administered before the training session, within fifteen days of training all but one achieved a stable level of 75 per cent or more on five successive days. In five students out of six there was substantial generalization of skills to the classroom environment. They also had an average improvement of 37 percentile points in their ranking in the classroom, in relation to other students in the same grade. On three of the four transfer tests that were administered the students demonstrated significant improvements.

In the third and final study it was decided to provide the instruction in the realistic, naturally occurring circumstances of a regular school classroom, with classroom teachers giving the training. The study was preceded by three sessions in which the teachers were carefully taught to follow the procedures used in the earlier studies. Then the teachers taught their students, in four groups ranging in numbers from four to seven.

The results of the third study were very similar to the earlier findings. There were large and reliable improvements in comprehension, according to each of a number of separate measures. The small decline in comprehension scores that occurred after a six-month period was rapidly remedied in just one training session. The training also transferred successfully to comprehension skills other than those that were taught.

Some Conclusions

The authors of the above studies consider some of the possible reasons for the success of their training procedures, in contrast to other training studies that have failed to produce durable improvements. First, they point out, the training was extensive: it involved a considerable amount of time and effort. Secondly, the particular skills that were taught were ones that had been carefully specified in the context of a theoretical account of comprehension processes. A lack of such skills was known to cause problems for poor readers. Third, the training was tailored to the needs of the particular students. These individuals were able to carry out the decoding skills required for reading but they lacked the active skills necessary for effective comprehension. Fourth, the skills chosen were ones that could be expected to be useful in a variety of different learning situations. Also, emphasis was placed on making sure that students did understand the importance of the skills and activities they learned in the training sessions. Finally, the interactive dialogue context provided a number of useful advantages over alternative ways of teaching.

The research that has been described in the present chapter demonstrates that carefully designed training which is based on a knowledge of the skills that underlie the ability to learn from the written word can produce large and genuine improvements. It is not at all easy to bring about substantial increases in comprehension, but the research findings show that it can be done.

In other chapters we have described numerous findings demonstrating that it is possible to improve students' performance in many of the sub-skills that are needed for classroom learning tasks. An especially valuable feature of the present series of studies is that they show that it is also possible to devise training procedures in which such skills are taught together in a co-ordinated fashion. This results in striking practical gains in the ability to understand written materials.

9

Extending Writing Skills

Having examined ways to help students learn from written materials, we now turn to looking at techniques that contribute to the ability to produce information in written form. The production of prose descriptions by young writers requires most of the skills necessary for understanding texts, but it also demands other abilities, and it is more difficult.

From Conversation to Written Communication

Most children are reasonably effective at giving descriptions in spoken language. Written communication draws upon many of the language abilities we use in talking to other people, but communicating in writing is harder. That is largely because the writer has to manage without the many verbal and non-verbal aids to communication that people can depend on when they talk to each other. For example, in a conversation each partner can help the other in a variety of ways. They can signal to the other person when to proceed, when to stop, when repetition of a point or further explanation is required, when to move to another topic, and indicate when full understanding depends upon additional information being provided (Bereiter and Scardamalia, 1982; see also Smith and Elley, 1998). The listener's need for additional information may be communicated through body language – a puzzled stare, a nod of the head – or through words, for instance, in a question such as 'But how did you get there in the first place?'

With written communication none of these aids is present. The writer has to be completely explicit. It may be necessary to plan the narrative in advance in order to include all the required information. Many people never gain the ability to express themselves clearly in writing. Indeed, among all the achievements that school learning promotes, written communication is arguably both the most valuable and the hardest to master.

The young writer has to learn to combine a number of different skills. In the present chapter we examine two particular capabilities that students can utilize in written communications. These are, first, note-taking, and second, making summaries. We also consider additional ways in which students can be helped to acquire other abilities that can play a direct part in the process of making written accounts.

Note-taking

The most obviously useful outcome of taking notes is to provide a convenient record of needed information. As it happens, the content of students' notes is often somewhat inaccurate, as Hartley and Cameron (1967) observed. However, there are other outcomes of taking notes that have positive implications for students' progress as learners.

1   The first advantage arises from the fact that the activity of taking notes, which is undertaken when a student is either listening to the teacher or reading a text passage, may help the learner attend to the material being studied. It is by no means always easy to give sustained attention to information to be learned, especially when it is difficult: any activity that can make it easier for a student to attend may prove beneficial. There are wide variations between students in the amount of time they spend actively engaged on school tasks. Attentiveness, indicated by the amount of a student's time that is actively directed towards learning tasks, is positively correlated with school achievement (Bloom, 1974; Glaser, 1982).

2   Secondly, it is possible that a student who, as a result of taking

notes, provides himself or herself with a form of the material that is in that individual's own words thereby acquires a version of the information that is especially clear or meaningful to the particular individual who made the notes.

3   Thirdly, the actual mental processing and coding activities that occur when a student takes notes may have direct effects upon learning. As we observed in chapter 3, there is ample evidence that the mental processing that takes place when careful attention is given to the meaning of information has strong positive influences upon learning.

In practice, it is not easy to disentangle these three positive outcomes of taking notes, but it is clear that taking notes does influence learning. It has useful outcomes apart from just making a record of needed information. One experiment by the author (Howe, 1970) was designed to investigate the connections between individual students' note-taking activities and subsequent learning. Students were asked to listen to a prose passage and take notes on it. They were told to keep the notes brief but to try to retain the important elements in the passage. Immediately afterwards they gave their notes to the experimenter (and they were unable to use the notes later for revision purposes). One week afterwards there was a recall test, in which the students were asked to write down whatever they could remember of the content of the original passage.

When the students' attempts at recall were scored, it was found that, on average, they remembered around 4 of the 20 meaningful parts of the passage. The experimenter was especially interested in discovering the relationship between the detailed content of each student's attempt at recall and the content of the same person's notes. Inspection of the notes revealed that the average number of the 20 meaningful elements from the text that appeared in an individual's notes was 10.8. The question of particular interest was, what is the relationship between an item from the passage being recorded in a person's notes and that same person remembering the item?

For each individual student, considering only those items which that person had recorded in his or her notes, the probability of such an item also being recalled in the test administered a week afterwards was, on average, one in three. But the probability of an item that did not appear in an individual's notes being recalled was very much lower, only one in twenty. In other words, the likelihood of a particular item being recalled was very strongly influenced by whether that same item had been recorded in the student's notes. That happened despite the fact that, since the notes were taken away from the students immediately after they had been made, there was no opportunity for a student to consult them before the recall test.

There are a number of possible reasons for the contents of students' notes and the same individuals' recall attempts being so closely related. It is possible, for instance, that taking notes on some items in a passage makes it difficult for the listener to attend to other parts. Also, the particular items that appear in a student's notes may partly reflect that individual's judgement about the relative importance of the different parts of the text, and the same judgements may also affect recall. In any case, despite any uncertainties concerning the detailed explanation of the findings, it is clear that attentional processes are involved. Certainly, the particular ways in which individuals direct their note-taking activities have powerful effects in determining what is actually learned.

Effects of Repeated Recall Attempts

The above note-taking study provides a down-to-earth demonstration of the principle that was described in chapter 3, namely that whatever students actively *do* (mentally) and what they learn are closely connected. However, combining this observation with the known tendency for previous knowledge to influence remembering of new events, sometimes adversely (as discussed in chapter 5), introduces the possibility that mistaken versions of events that are produced by inaccurate note-taking or related activities may be hard to eradicate. That possibility was investigated in a further experiment.

Students listened to a passage taken from a novel, and afterwards they tried to recall the information. An unusual feature about this study was that the students listened to the passage and subsequently tried to recall it on several separate occasions. Following their attempt to remember the passage they listened to it (that is, the correct version) again, and a week later they were asked to try once again to recall it. Again, the passage was presented once more afterwards. A week after that, the students again attempted recall, and once again they listened to the original passage. In all, there were four presentations of the same passage, and the students made four separate attempts to recall it.

The findings concerning overall accuracy of remembering in the successive sessions did not yield any great surprises. A more striking aspect of the results was that there was only a rather small increase in accuracy of remembering from week to week: recall rose from around 8 out of 20 meaningful segments in the first test to around 12 out of 20 in the final test.

Much more remarkable, however, were the findings that emerged from an examination of the detailed contents of individuals' successive attempts to recall the passage from one week to the next. On each of these occasions, the actual information that each particular student remembered from the passage was extremely similar. That is to say, the students were extremely good at remembering exactly what they had recalled on the previous recall tests (and at remembering any errors that they had introduced on previous occasions). Conversely, they were not at all successful at either remembering information from the passage which they had not previously recalled or at correcting previous errors. That was despite the fact that the correct original version of the passage was presented on four separate occasions, and on each occasion the students were visibly interested in spotting their mistakes and trying to ensure that they would now retain the correct version of the passage. It appears that once a learner had recalled something wrongly, it was very difficult to correct the (incorrect) version retained in memory.

Despite all the students' efforts, it appeared that they learned much less from the repetitions of the correct versions than from their own mental activity involved in trying to remember the information. For instance, if a meaningful item was recalled on each of the first three attempts, the probability of that one being recalled correctly again on the fourth trial was very high, 0.98, but the probability of an item that was not recalled on the first three tests being remembered on the fourth was very low, only 0.2. This was despite the fact that subjects had by that stage listened to the original passage on no less than four occasions. Note also that these probabilities refer to the number of meaningful ideas remembered and not to the literal recall of particular words.

This finding has a definite implication for classroom teaching, as well as providing a further demonstration that what students learn largely depends upon what they do. It is not uncommon for teachers to give students a test and later go over the correct answers, on the assumption that after students have been told the correct answers to the questions they will subsequently remember them. The present findings indicate that such an assumption is ill-founded. In reality, it appears, students are much more likely to go on remembering their own wrong answers to the test questions. As Robert Glaser (1982) has noted, we need to be cautious about agreeing with the view that 'practice makes perfect.' It usually does, of course, but it is also not uncommon for children to unwittingly practise errors and misconceptions, in which event their practising will not lead to useful learning.

Simply being told the right answer to a question is not enough to ensure that it will be retained. What is required is some procedure whereby the student is able to arrive at the correct answer for himself, even if this necessitates a fair amount of effort and retracing of earlier steps. Precisely how that is best achieved will depend on the particular circumstances. However, it is important to ensure that the mental processing involved (or 'mental effort') is at least as deep and extensive as the mental activity that originally led to the student remembering an incorrect version of the information.

Note-taking Style and Student Learning

To return to taking notes as such, the author's research (Howe, 1970) has also shown that what a student note-taker actually learns from the material on which the notes are made may be related to the manner in which notes were initially made. In the note-taking study described earlier, the investigator counted the number of words that appeared in each student's notes, and also counted the number of meaningful ideas from the passage that were successfully communicated in those notes.

The ratio obtained by dividing the number of ideas successfully recorded by the number of words that an individual student needed to record can be regarded as an indication of the efficiency of that student's note-taking approach. That is because it is a measure of the extent to which that student was successful in communicating a large amount of meaningful content in few words. And the calculated ratio also gives a rough indication of the extent to which the student transformed the original passage into his or her own words.

The question is, does a relationship exist between such ratios and students' actual learning, as measured by their scores on the test of recall administered a week after the information was originally presented (at which time they made their notes)? The answer is positive. There was a positive correlation (+0.5) between individual students' ratios (obtained by dividing the number of ideas in their notes by the number of words they used to express those ideas) and their recall of the information in the prose passage.

This finding does not by itself prove that individual differences in note-taking practices cause differences in learning. The fact that there was a correlation between the two measures could have been due to the fact that the mental activities necessary for taking effective notes are ones that also lead to accurate retention. Nevertheless, it is useful to have our attention drawn to the fact that measures of the outcomes of note-taking activities (in common with various other kinds of activities, as we have seen) and measures of how much students learn are definitely related to each other. This is yet more evidence of links between learning and learners' mental activities.

Note also that in normal classroom circumstances, any differences in the effectiveness for learning of note-taking activities as such are compounded by differences in the value of the notes that are actually produced. Pupils typically make extensive use of their own notes, for revision and other purposes. At this stage it is undoubtedly useful to have good notes, in which the required information is effectively recorded.

Using Pre-prepared Notes

Some teachers dictate notes to their students or provide them with notes that the teacher has prepared. Doing that can be a convenient way of enabling students to have a written version of required information. However, that is achieved at the cost of depriving students of the benefits of making notes for themselves. In some situations, but not in others, the added convenience of pre-prepared notes may compensate for that.

In certain instances it may be sensible to encourage students to take notes for themselves but to provide extra notes at a later stage for those individuals who require them. In one study (Howe and Godfrey, 1977), British students at a sixth-form college were asked to listen to and take notes on a somewhat rambling and unorganized historical passage describing an early Chinese dynasty. Afterwards they were tested for recall of the passage contents. Then some of the students were told to revise from their own notes, while the other students were provided with a version of the information that was much more clearly organized than the passage of text they had listened to. Later, all the students were tested again for long-term retention of the information.

The most interesting finding was that giving students the organized written version of the text helped some students considerably, but others did not benefit at all. Those students who performed relatively well in the original test did not benefit from being provided with the highly organized version that had been prepared for them. That is to say, for those students whose original test scores were in the top quarter, subsequent test performance was no better if they were given the organized version than if they had to revise from the notes they had made for themselves.

However, for students who did badly in the original recall test, giving them the organized version of the material brought considerable advantages. These students (whose initial test scores were in the bottom quarter) subsequently performed much better if they were able to use the organized version than if they had to rely on their own notes.

Clearly, the procedure of giving students a highly organized written version of the material to be learned was a very helpful one for some but not at all useful for others. This finding serves as a useful reminder that in most school learning situations the value of a particular method or procedure depends greatly upon its appropriateness for the particular learners who use it. A procedure that is extremely useful for some students may be much less so for others.

Learning to Make Notes

Like any other skill, note-taking needs to be learned. All too often it is assumed that by the time students reach a certain age they have somehow acquired the capability to make notes without ever having received instruction in how to do so.

To be effective at taking notes, an individual has to record important items of information but without wasting time and effort in writing down non-essential items. This takes practice. For the child who is beginning to learn to take notes two kinds of preparatory activities can be particularly useful. The first is simply to underline the important words in a passage that the child is reading. This provides needed experience that helps a learner to gain expertise in detecting which are the most important words in a passage of text.

The kind of 'dialogue' learning situation that was mentioned in connection with comprehension skills can be particularly effective for helping children to identify the important parts of a text passage. For example, teacher and child can take turns in going through a passage and underlining the important words, at the same time saying why they are important. There is some evidence that simply underlining important items can have a positive effect on learning prose materials: it was found in one study that underlining improved students' learning of information from a 6,000-word text passage.

The second and slightly more difficult preparatory exercise for children who are beginning to learn how to take notes involves actually writing down the most important words. For instance, a child might be asked to write down the three most important words in each sentence. Again, it is also useful to ask the children to say why they think that particular words are especially important. That can help them to acquire the sub-skill of detecting those words that are most crucial. Like underlining, writing down important words can itself aid learning. In one study (Howe and Godfrey, 1977) it was discovered that students who were told to record the three words that they considered most important in each sentence of a prose passage recalled the passage as accurately as students who tried to write down the entire text. Those students who were successful in choosing crucial words recalled more items than students whose word choices were less appropriate.

Making Summaries

The ability to make summaries draws upon similar skills to those involved in note-taking. Summarizing is often valuable, and being able to do that is essential for students who need to produce written reports, compositions and essays. But, as with note-taking, while the value of summarizing is widely acknowledged, children are not often provided with systematic instruction aimed at helping them to make summaries of texts.

Jeanne Day has listed five simple rules for students to follow in making summaries (Brown and Day, 1983), as follows:

1 Delete unimportant information. A summary should not contain information that is trivial.
2 Delete redundant information. Summaries should not be repetitive.
3 Use subordinates in place of lists of items.
4 If possible, 'lift' from the passage a topic sentence stating the main theme, and put it in the summary.
5 If there is no topic sentence, make one up for the summary.

Setting out definite rules to follow is often helpful for young students. By the age of 12 most children can use the first three of the above rules with little or no instruction. The others are more difficult, but training was effective in improving students' performance at making summaries. Day taught summarizing skills to students of varying ability. For all the students, rules 4 and 5 were the most difficult to put into practice, but all except the least capable of the young people were eventually able to follow all five rules.

Learning Other Skills that Aid Writing: Remedial Activities

In learning how to write effectively it is necessary to combine and co-ordinate a variety of skills. Because a number of different skills are involved, most of them dependent on each other, writing may seem to be an impossible task for the beginner. As one leading researcher into children's writing, Marlene Scardamalia, remarks,

> To pay conscious attention to handwriting, spelling, punctuation, word choice, syntax, textual connections, purpose, organization, clarity, rhythm, euphony, and reader characteristics would seemingly overload the information processing capacity of the best intellects. For the skilled writer we may suppose that many aspects of writing are automated and that cognitive space-saving strategies make writing possible without inordinate demands on processing capacity. For the beginning writer, however, very little is automated and coping strategies are lacking. (Scardamalia, 1981, p. 81)

Nevertheless, Scardamalia observes, most children do learn to write, and some even enjoy it. The necessary abilities are not acquired quickly or easily, but over a period of years children do gradually become increasingly successful at expressing their thoughts in writing.

At the beginning of the chapter we mentioned some of the demands of writing that are not encountered in spoken language, for example, in a conversation. Some of the particular problems that a child meets in progressing from conversation to written conversation have been summarized by Bereiter and Scardamalia (1982), who also identify suitable intervention that teachers can introduce in order to overcome the problems.

Inadequate quantity of text

First, there are a number of problems that a child runs into when learning to generate text in the absence of a conversational partner or respondent. For example, the quantity of text that a young child may produce may be limited to the length of a single turn in a conversation, and that is likely to be insufficient for writing purposes.

In this event, it is suggested that a teacher should merely prompt the child to 'say more'. Simple interventions of this kind can lead to large increases in the quantity of text produced, with no deterioration of quality. Another suggested procedure is to ask the child to produce a kind of 'slow dictation'. This involves producing language orally, without the mechanical burden of having to write things down. Again, such interventions have proved successful in helping children to produce prose passages that are considerably longer than is usual in face-to-face conversation.

Not knowing what to write

Secondly, children can have problems in knowing what to write, even when they are prompted to produce more. They need help in order to learn how to search their own memories for suitable content.

Bereiter and Scardamalia have had success with a number of procedures for helping children to overcome this source of difficulty. One device is to supply prompts that provide 'openers' for sentences, but stopping short of cueing specific information. For example, the researchers tried giving children a set of openers such as 'I think . . . ', 'For example . . . ' and 'Even though . . .' For many children aged between 9 and 14 these openers can be helpful for increasing written output.

Lack of planning

A third kind of problem encountered in going from conversational to written expression is that much more planning is necessary. In young children, planning may be limited to decisions about 'What shall I say next?' and this may be decided by writing down anything that comes to mind which is related to the topic. Thus:

> A common composition tactic of young writers is to tell all they know on a topic irrespective of the writing assignment. For example, when writing an essay on winter, the child might begin with 'I think winter is the best time of year because you can make snowmen'; the child will then proceed for many more sentences telling all she knows about snowmen. Having exhausted that topic, the child will declare that the composition is ended, seemingly having 'forgotten' the original purpose of the essay. (Brown and Day, 1983, p. 13)

Children's planning tends to lack the 'attention to the whole' that is found in mature people's written compositions. Young writers frequently proceed one step at a time without much organization in advance.

Bereiter and Scardamalia introduced a number of techniques for helping children learn to make plans. One involved giving children final sentences, and telling them to build their compositions towards those endings. For example, in one training session 12-year-olds had to make up a story that ended with the sentence, 'And so, after considering the reasons for it and the reasons against it, the duke decided to rent his castle to the vampire after all, in spite of the rumour he had heard.'

Given this task, the children worked together on a plan for the story. They did not find it at all easy, but they soon realized that it was necessary to think of reasons for and against the decision to rent the castle, and the children eventually made progress towards finding a solution that made a good story. Discussing the planning problems in a group provides useful opportunities for children to learn to achieve the kinds of planning that a writer must eventually do alone.

Although it takes people time and effort to improve their writing skills, progress can normally be made as soon as the nature of the difficulties being experienced has been identified. As with other skills, it is particularly helpful for a writer to know precisely what he or she is aiming for, and a complicating factor in writing is that there are often a number of separate aims to be considered at the same time. It may be reassuring to know that even the most expert writers and authors have had to struggle, and their capacity to write fluently and with apparent ease is possible only because they have spent years improving their capabilities. Famous authors such as Charles Dickens and the Brontës devoted large amounts of time to sharpening their writing skills; only gradually did they gain the remarkable expertise for which they are justly admired.

References

Amabile, T. M. (1983). *The Social Psychology of Creativity*. New York: Springer-Verlag.

Atkinson, R. C. (1975). Mnemotechnics in second-language learning. *American Psychologist*, 30, 821–8.

Ausubel, D. P. (1968). *Educational Psychology: a cognitive view*. New York: Holt, Rinehart & Winston.

Bandura, A. (1986). *Social Foundations of Thought and Action*. Englewood Cliffs, NJ: Prentice-Hall.

Bartlett, F. C. (1932). *Remembering*. Cambridge: Cambridge University Press.

Bates, J. A. (1979). Extrinsic reward and intrinsic motivation: a review with implications for the classroom. *Review of Educational Research*, 49, 557–76.

Belmont, J. M. (1978). Individual differences in memory: the cases of normal and retarded development. In M. M. Gruneberg and P. E. Morris (eds), *Aspects of Memory*. London: Methuen, 153–85.

Benjamin, H. (1939). *The Sabre-Tooth Curriculum*. New York: McGraw-Hill.

Bereiter, C. and Scardamalia, M. (1982). From conversation to composition: the role of instruction in a developmental process. In R. Glaser (ed.), *Advances in Instructional Psychology*, vol. 2. Hillsdale, NJ: Erlbaum, 1–64.

Bloom, B. S. (1974). Time and learning. *American Psychologist*, 29, 682–8.

Bloom, B. S. (ed.) (1956). *Taxonomy of Educational Objectives. Handbook One: cognitive domain*. New York: David McKay.

Bower, G. H. and Clark, M. C. (1969). Narrative stories as mediators of serial learning. *Psychonomic Science*, 14, 181–2.

Bower, G. H. and Karlin, M. B. (1974). Depth of processing pictures of faces and recognition memory. *Journal of Experimental Psychology*, 103, 751–7.

Bradley, L. and Bryant, P. E. (1983). Categorizing sounds and learning to read in preschoolers. *Journal of Educational Psychology*, 68, 680–8.

Brainerd, C. J. (1977). Cognitive development and concept learning: an interpretative review. *Psychological Bulletin*, 84, 919–39.

Bransford, J. D., Nitsch, K. E. and Franks, J. J. (1977). Schooling and the facilitation of knowing. In R. C. Anderson, R. J. Spiro and W. E. Montague (eds), *Schooling and the Acquisition of Knowledge*. Hillsdale, NJ: Erlbaum, 31–64.

Bransford, J. D., Stein, B. S., Shelton, T. S. and Owings, R. A. (1981). Cognition and adaptation: the importance of learning to learn. In J. H. Harvey (ed.), *Cognition, Social Behavior, and the Environment*. Hillsdale, NJ: Erlbaum, 93–110.

Brewer, W. F. and Dupree, D. A. (1983). Use of plan schemata in the recall and recognition of goal-directed actions. *Journal of Experimental Psychology: Learning, Memory, and Cognition*, 9, 117–29.

Brown, A. L. and Day, J. D. (1983). Macrorules for summarizing texts: the development of expertise. *Journal of Verbal Learning and Verbal Behavior*, 22, 1–14.

Brown, A. L., Palincsar, A. S. and Armbruster, B. B. (1984). Instructing comprehension-fostering activities in interactive learning situations. In H. Mandl, N. Stein and T. Trabasso (eds), *Learning and Comprehension of Texts*. Hillsdale, NJ: Erlbaum.

Brown, A. L. and Smiley, S. S. (1978). The development of strategies for studying texts. *Child Development*, 49, 1076–88.

Bruner, J. S. (1972). Nature and uses of immaturity. *American Psychologist*, 27, 687–707.

Bryant, P. and Bradley, L. (1985). *Children's Reading Problems: psychology and education*. Oxford: Blackwell.

Ceci, S. J. (1990). *On Intelligence . . . More or Less: a bio-ecological treatise on intellectual development*. Englewood Cliffs, NJ: Prentice-Hall.

Ceci, S. J., Caves, R. T. and Howe, M. J. A. (1981). Children's long-term memory for information that is incongruous with their prior knowledge. *British Journal of Psychology*, 72, 443–50.

Ceci, S. J. and Howe, M. J. A. (1978). Semantic knowledge as a determinant of developmental differences in recall. *Journal of Experimental Child Psychology*, 26, 230–45.

Ceci, S. J. and Liker, J. (1986). A day at the races: a study of IQ, expertise, and cognitive complexity. *Journal of Experimental Psychology: General*, 115, 255–66.

Chi, M. T. H. (1978). Knowledge structures and memory development.

In R. Siegler (ed.), *Children's Thinking: what develops?* Hillsdale, NJ: Erlbaum, 73–96.

Chi, M. T. H. and Koeske, R. D. (1983). Network representation of a child's dinosaur knowledge. *Developmental Psychology*, 19, 29–39.

Clarke, A. M. and Clarke, A. D. B. (1976). *Early Experience: myth and evidence.* London: Open Books.

Cloward, R. D. (1967). Studies in tutoring. *Journal of Experimental Education*, 36, 14–25.

Coles, G. (1987). *The Learning Mystique.* New York: Fawcett Ballantine.

Collier, G. (1994). *Social Origins of Mental Ability.* New York: Wiley.

Collins, A. and Quillian, M. R. (1969). Retrieval time from semantic memory. *Journal of Verbal Learning and Verbal Behavior*, 8, 240–7.

—— (1972). How to make a language user. In E. Tulving and W. Donaldson (eds), *Organization of Memory.* New York: Academic Press, 310–54.

Collins, A. and Smith, E. E. 1982. Teaching the process of reading comprehension. In D. K. Detterman and R. J. Sternberg (eds), *How and How Much can Intelligence be Increased?* Norwood, NJ: Ablex, 173–86.

Conrad, C. (1972). Cognitive economy in semantic memory. *Journal of Experimental Psychology*, 92, 149–54.

Covington, M. L. and Omelich, C. L. (1981). As failures mount: affective and cognitive consequences of ability demotion in the classroom. *Journal of Educational Psychology*, 73, 796–808.

Craik, F. I. M. and Lockhart, R. S. (1972). Levels of processing: a framework for memory research. *Journal of Verbal Learning and Verbal Behavior*, 12, 599–607.

Craik, F. I. M. and Tulving, E. (1975). Depth of processing and the retention of words in episodic memory. *Journal of Experimental Psychology: General*, 104, 268–94.

Csikszentmihalyi, M. and Csikszentmihalyi, I. S. (1993). Family influences on the development of giftedness. In G. R. Bock and K. Ackrill (eds), *CIBA Foundation Symposium 178: The Origins and Development of High Ability.* Chichester: Wiley, 187–206.

Deacon, T. (1997). *The Symbolic Species.* London: Allen Lane/The Penguin Press.

de Charms, R. (1976). *Enhancing Motivation: change in the classroom.* New York: Halsted.

Donaldson, M. (1978). *Children's Minds.* London: Fontana.

Dooling, D. J. and Lachman, R. (1971). Effects of comprehension on retention of prose. *Journal of Experimental Psychology*, 88, 216–22.

Duchastel, P. C. (1982). Testing effects measured with alternate test forms. *Educational Research*, 75, 309–13.

Dunn, J. and Plomin, R. (1990). *Separate Lives: why siblings are so different*. New York: Basic Books.

Durkin, H. (1995). *Developmental Social Psychology*. Oxford: Blackwell.

Ericsson, K. A. and Charness, N. (1994). Expert performance: its structure and acquisition. *American Psychologist*, 49, 725–47.

Ericsson, K. A., Krampe, R. Th. and Tesch-Römer, C. (1995). The role of deliberate practice in the acquisition of expert performance. *Psychological Review*, 100, 363–406.

Escalona, S. K. (1973). The differential impact of environmental conditions as a function of different reaction patterns in infancy. In J. C. Westman (ed.), *Individual Differences in Children*. New York: Wiley.

Estes, W. K. (1970). *Learning Theory and Mental Development*. New York: Academic Press.

Feuerstein, R. (1979). *The Dynamic Assessment of Retarded Performers: the learning potential assessment device, theory, instruments, and techniques*. Baltimore, MD: University Park Press.

Flavell, J. H., Beach, D. R. and Chinsky, J. M. (1966). Spontaneous verbal rehearsal in a memory task as a function of age. *Child Development*, 37, 324–40.

Flynn, J. R. (1987). Massive IQ gains in 14 nations: what IQ tests really measure. *Psychological Bulletin*, 101, 271–91.

—— (1991). *Asian Americans: achievement beyond IQ*. Hillsdale, NJ: Erlbaum.

Fontana, D. (1981). *Psychology for Teachers*. London: British Psychological Society/Macmillan.

Fowler, W. (1990). Early stimulation and the development of verbal talents. In M. J. A. Howe (ed.), *Encouraging the Development of Exceptional Abilities and Talent*. Leicester: British Psychological Society, 179–210.

Gagne, R. M. (1968). Contributions of learning to human development. *Journal of Educational Psychology*, 60, 408–14.

Garber, J., Braafledt, N. and Zeman, J. (1991). The regulation of sad effect: an information-processing perspective. In J. Garber and K. A. Dodge (eds), *The Development of Emotion*. Cambridge: Cambridge University Press.

Gardner, H. (1995). Cracking open the IQ box. In S. Fraser (ed.), *The Bell Curve Wars: race, intelligence, and the future of America*. New York: Basic Books, 23–35.

Gates, A. I. (1917). Recitation as a factor in memorizing. *Archives of Psychology*, 6, no. 40.

Glaser, R. (1982). Instructional psychology: past, present and future. *American Psychologist*, 37, 292–305.

Goldstein, D. M. (1976). Cognitive–linguistic functioning and learning to read in preschoolers. *Journal of Educational Psychology*, 68, 680–8.

Gruneberg, M. M. (1973). The role of memorization techniques in finals examination preparation: a study of psychology students. *Educational Research*, 16, 134–9.

Hart, B. and Risley, T. (1995). *Meaningful Differences in Everyday Parenting and Intellectual Development in Young American Children*. Baltimore: Brookes.

Hartley, J. and Cameron, A. (1967). Some observations on the efficiency of lecturing. *Education Review*, 20, 30–7.

Hepper, P. G. (1991). An examination of fetal learning before and after birth. *Irish Journal of Psychology*, 12, 95–107.

Herrnstein, R. J. and Murray, C. (1994). *The Bell Curve: intelligence and class structure in American life*. New York: Free Press.

Howe, M. J. A. (1970). Repeated presentation and recall of meaningful prose. *Journal of Educational Psychology*, 61, 214–19.

—— (1975). *Learning in Infants and Young Children*. London: Macmillan.

—— (1977). Learning and the acquisition of knowledge by students: some experimental investigations. In M. J. A. Howe (ed.), *Adult Learning: psychological research and applications*. London: Wiley, 1–16.

—— (1980). *The Psychology of Human Learning*. New York: Harper & Row.

—— (1997). *IQ in Question: the truth about intelligence*. London: Sage.

—— (1998). Can IQ change? *Psychologist*, 11, 1–3.

Howe, M. J. A., Davidson, J. W. and Sloboda, J. A. (1998). Innate talents: reality or myth? *Behavioral and Brain Sciences*, 21, 399–442.

Howe, M. J. A., Davidson, J. W., Moore, D .G. and Sloboda, J. A. (1995). Are there early signs of musical ability? *Psychology of Music*, 23, 162–76.

Howe, M. J. A. and Godfrey, J. (1977). *Student Note-taking as an Aid to Learning*. Exeter: Exeter University Teaching Services.

Hyde, T. S. and Jenkins, J. J. (1969. Differential effects of incidental tasks on the organization of recall of a list of highly associated words. *Journal of Experimental Psychology*, 82, 472–81.

Jensen, A. R. (1978). The nature of intelligence and its relation to learning. In S. Murray-Smith (ed.), *Melbourne Studies in Education*. Melbourne: Melbourne University Press.

Karmiloff-Smith, A. (1995) The extraordinary cognitive journey from foetus through infancy. *Journal of Child Psychology and Psychiatry*, 36, 1293–313.

Kasper, L. F. 1983. The effect of linking sentence and interactive picture mnemonics on the acquisition of Spanish nouns by middle school children. *Human Learning: Journal of Practical Research and Applications*, 2, 141–56.

Kintsch, W. (1975). Memory for prose. In C. N. Cofer (ed.), *The Structure of Human Memory*. San Francisco: Freeman, 90–113.

Korner, A. F. (1971). Individual differences at birth: implications for early experience and later development. *American Journal of Orthopsychiatry*, 41, 608–19.

Lakoff, G. and Johnson, M. (1980). *Metaphors We Live By*. Chicago: University of Chicago Press.

Levin, J. R., McCormick, C. B., Miller, G. E., Berry, J. K. and Pressley, M. (1982). Mnemonic versus non-mnemonic vocabulary learning strategies for children. *American Educational Research Journal*, 19, 121–36.

Loftus, E. F. and Palmer, J. C. (1974). Reconstruction of automobile destruction: an example of the interaction between language and memory. *Journal of Verbal Learning and Verbal Behavior*, 13, 585–9.

McClelland, D. C. (1973). Testing for competence rather than for 'intelligence'. *American Psychologist*, 28, 1–14.

Markman, E. (1979). Realizing that you don't understand: elementary school children's awareness of inconsistencies. *Child Development*, 50, 643–55.

Marton, F. (1981). Phenomenography – describing conceptions of the world around us. *Instructional Science*, 10, 177–200.

Matheny, K. and Edwards, C. (1974). Academic improvement through an experimental classroom management system. *Journal of School Psychology*, 12, 222–32.

Meadows, S. (1996). *Parenting Behaviour and Children's Cognitive Development*. Hove: Psychology Press.

Moon, C. and Wells, G. (1979). The influence of home on learning to read. *Journal of Research in Reading*, 2, 53–62.

Morris, P. E., Tweedy, M. and Gruneberg, M. M. (1985). Interest, knowledge and the memorizing of soccer scores. *British Journal of Psychology*, 76, 415–25.

Pressley, G. M. (1977). Children's use of the keyword method to learn simple Spanish vocabulary words. *Journal of Educational Psychology*, 69, 465–72.

Raugh, M. R. and Atkinson, R. C. (1975). A mnemonic method for learning a second language vocabulary. *Journal of Educational Psychology*, 67, 1–16.

Renninger, K. A. and Wozniak, R. N. (1985). Effect of interest on attentional shift, recognition and recall in young children. *Developmental Psychology*, 21, 624–32.

Rips, L. J., Shoben, E. J. and Smith, E. E. (1973). Semantic distance and the verification of semantic relations. *Journal of Verbal Learning and Verbal Behaviour*, 12, 1–20.

Rogers, T. B., Kuiper, N. A. and Kirker, W. S. (1977). Self-references and the encoding of personal information. *Journal of Personality and Social Psychology*, 38, 677–88.

Rothkopf, E. Z. (1970). The concept of mathemagenic activities. *Review of Educational Research*, 40, 325–36.

Rotter, J. (1975). Some problems and misconceptions related to the construct of internal versus external control of reinforcement. *Journal of Consulting and Clinical Psychology*, 43, 56–67.

Scardamalia, M. (1981). How children cope with the cognitive demands of writing. In C. H. Frederikson and J. F. Dominic (eds), *Writing: the nature, development and teaching of written communication*, vol. 2 . Hillsdale, NJ: Erlbaum, 81–104.

Schaffer, H. R. and Emerson, P. E. (1964). Patterns of response to physical contact in early human development. *Journal of Child Psychology and Psychiatry*, 5, 1–13.

Schank, R. C. and Abelson, R. P. (1977). *Scripts, Plans, Goals, and Understanding: an inquiry into human knowledge structures*. Hillsdale, NJ: Erlbaum.

Scribner, S. (1984). Studying working intelligence. In B. Rogoff and J. Lave (eds), *Everyday Cognition: its development in social context*. Cambridge, MA: Harvard University Press.

Seligman, M. E. P. (1975). *Helplessness: on depression, development and death*. San Francisco: Freeman.

Shoda, Y., Mischel, W. and Peake, P. K (1990). Predicting adolescent cognitive and self-regulatory competences from preschool delay of gratification. *Developmental Psychology*, 26 (6), 978–86.

Slater, A. M. (1995). Individual differences in infancy and later IQ. *Journal of Child Psychology and Psychiatry*, 36, 69–112.

Sloboda, J. A., Davidson, J. W. and Howe, M. J. A. (1994). Is everyone musical? *Psychologist*, 7, 349–54.

Sloboda, J. A., Davidson, J. W., Howe, M. J. A. and Moore, D. G. (1996).

The role of practice in the development of performing musicians. *British Journal of Psychology*, 87, 287–309, 399–412.

Sloboda, J. A. and Howe, M. J. A. (1991). Biographical precursors of musical excellence: an interview study. *Psychology of Music*, 19, 3–21.

Smith, J. and Elley, W. (1998). *How Children Learn to Write*. London: Chapman & Hall.

Snyder, M. and Uranowitz, S. W. (1978). Reconstructing the past: some cognitive consequences of person perception. *Journal of Personality and Social Psychology*, 36, 940–60.

Sosniak, L. A. (1985). Learning to be a concert pianist. In B. S. Bloom (ed.), *Developing Talent in Young People*. New York: Ballantine, 19–67.

—— (1990). The tortoise, the hare, and the development of talent. In M. J. A. Howe (ed.), *Encouraging the Development of Exceptional Abilities and Talents*. Leicester: British Psychological Society, 149–64.

Starkes, J., Deakin, J., Allard, F., Hodges, N. and Hayes, A. (1996). Deliberate practice in sports: what is it anyway? In K. A. Ericsson (ed.), *The Road to Excellence: the acquisition of expert performance in the arts and sciences*. Mahwah, NJ: Erlbaum, 81–106.

Stipek, D. J. and Weisz, J. R. (1981). Perceived personal control and academic achievement. *Review of Educational Research*, 51, 101–37.

Sweeney, C. A. and Bellezza, F. S. (1982). Use of the keyword mnemonic in learning English vocabulary. *Human Learning: Journal of Practical Research and Applications*, 1, 155–64.

Thompson, R. F. (1976). The search for the engram. *American Psychologist*, 32, 209–27.

Thorndike, E. L. (1931). *Human Learning*. New York: Prentice-Hall.

Turnure, J., Buium, N. and Thurlow, M. (1976). The effectiveness of interrogatives for promoting verbal elaboration productivity in young children. *Child Development*, 11, 780–7.

Wachs, T. D. and Gruen, G. E. (1982). *Early Experience and Human Development*. New York: Plenum Press.

Wang, M. and Stiles, B. (1976). An investigation of children's concept of self-responsibility for their school learning. *American Educational Research Journal*, 13, 159–79.

Wells, C. G. (1981). Some antecedents of early educational attainment. *British Journal of Sociology of Education*, 2, 181–200.

White, B. L. (1971). *Human Infants: experience and psychological development*. Englewood Cliffs, NJ: Prentice-Hall.

White, R. T. (1979). Achievement, mastery, proficiency, competence. *Studies in Science Education*, 6, 1–22.

Whitehurst, G. J., Falco, F. L., Lonigan, C. J., Fischel, J. E., DeBaryshe, B. D., Valdez-Menchaca, M. C. and Caulfield, M. (1988). Accelerating language development through picture book reading. *Developmental Psychology*, 24, 552–9.

Whitehurst, G. J. and Valdez-Menchaca, M. C. (1988). What is the role of reinforcement in early language acquisition? *Child Development*, 59, 430–40.

Winner, E. (1996). *Gifted Children: myths and realities*. New York: Basic Books.

Index